Contents

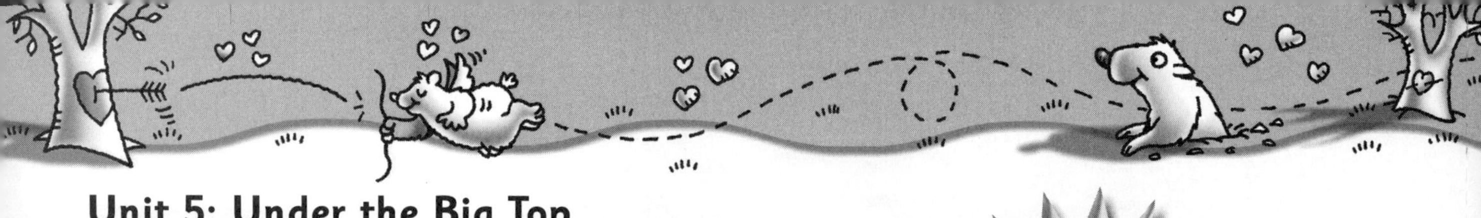

Unit 5: Under the Big Top

Unit 6: Let's Go Shopping!

Unit 7: Author Study— Anne Rockwell

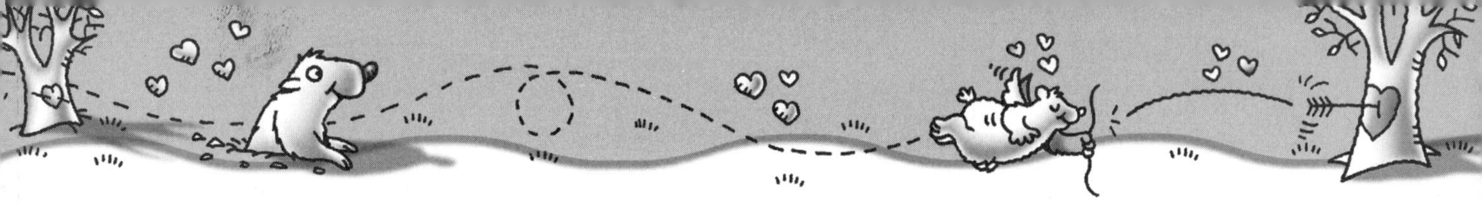

Introduction

This series of monthly activity books is designed to give PreK and Kindergarten teachers a collection of hands-on activities and ideas for each month of the year. The activities are standards-based and reflect the philosophy that children learn best through play. The teacher can use these ideas to enhance the development of language and math skills, and of social/emotional and physical growth of children. The opportunity to promote pre-reading skills is present throughout the series and should be incorporated whenever possible.

Organization and Features

Each book consists of seven units:

Unit 1 provides reproducible pages and information for the month in general.
- a newsletter outline to promote parent communication
- a blank thematic border page
- a list of special days in the month
- calendar ideas to promote math skills
- a blank calendar grid that can also be used as an incentive chart

Units 2–6 include an array of activities for five **theme** topics. Each unit includes
- teacher information on the theme
- arts and crafts ideas
- a food activity
- poetry, songs, and books
- bulletin board ideas
- center activities correlated to specific learning standards

Implement the activities in a way that best meets the needs of individual children.

Unit 7 focuses on a well-known **children's author**. The unit includes
- a biography of the author
- activities based on a literature selection
- a list of books by the author
- reproducible bookmarks

In addition, each book contains
- reproducible **icons** suitable to use as labels for centers in the classroom. The icons coordinate with the centers in the book. They may also be used with a work assignment chart to aid in assigning children to centers.
- reproducible **student awards**
- a **calendar day pattern** with suggested activities

Research Base

Howard Gardner's theory of multiple intelligences, or learning styles, validates teaching thematically and using a variety of approaches to help children learn. Providing a variety of experiences will assure that each child has an opportunity to learn in a comfortable way.

Following are the learning styles identified by Howard Gardner.
- **Verbal/Linguistic** learners need opportunities to read, listen, write, learn new words, and to tell stories.
- **Musical** learners enjoy music activities.
- **Logical/Mathematical** learners need opportunities to problem solve, count, measure, and do patterning activities.
- **Visual/Spatial** learners need opportunities to paint, draw, sculpt, and create art works.
- **Interpersonal** learners benefit from group discussions and group projects.
- **Intrapersonal** learners learn best in solitary activities, such as reading, writing in journals, and reflecting on information.
- **Naturalist** learners need opportunities to observe weather and nature and to take care of animals and plants.
- **Existential** learners can be fostered in the early years by asking children to think and respond, by discussions, and journal writing.

Gardner, H. (1994). *Frames of mind.* New York: Basic Books.

February News
Teacher:
Date:
Headline News
Coming Up
Happy Birthday to
Special Thanks to
Help Wanted

February

Special Days in February

American Heart Month Have children celebrate with activities from the Valentine's Day unit that begins on page 25.

Black History Month Explore the many contributions of African Americans and read *Only Passing Through* by Anne Rockwell.

National Cherry Month Eat cherries and play the game Hi Ho Cherrio.

President's Day (the third Monday in February) Explore the job of the President of the United States and discuss the importance of George Washington and Abraham Lincoln.

2 Groundhog Day Have children celebrate with activities from the Groundhogs unit that begins on page 10.

3 Carrot Cake Day Bake carrot cake muffins and serve them for snack.

6 Pay a Compliment Day Have children say a compliment to ten people during the day.

8 Kite Flying Day Fly a kite if the weather permits or have children decorate kite cutouts and add a tail made of yarn.

10 Umbrella Day Invite children to bring an umbrella to school. During recess on the playground, name characteristics of the umbrellas, such as a color or size. Children whose umbrellas fit the category twirl their umbrellas.

12 Lincoln's Birthday Share information about Abraham Lincoln. Then make a log cabin by gluing pretzel sticks to a cabin outline drawn on paper.

14 Valentine's Day Have children celebrate with activities from the Valentine's Day unit that begins on page 25.

20 National Hoodie-Hoo Day At noon, go outside and yell "hoodie-hoo" to scare winter away and encourage spring to arrive.

22 Washington's Birthday Share information about George Washington. Have children look at coins and paper money to find which ones show his image.

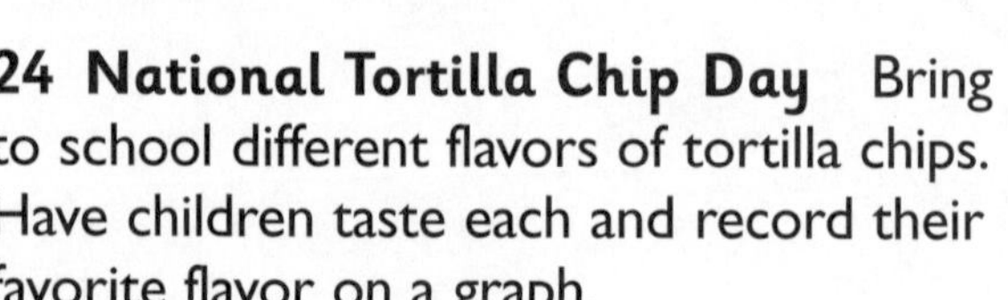

24 National Tortilla Chip Day Bring to school different flavors of tortilla chips. Have children taste each and record their favorite flavor on a graph.

29 Leap Day Explain the reason for Leap Day. Then set two ropes on the floor and have children leap over them. Increase the space between the ropes. Challenge children to see who can leap the greatest distance.

February

Sunday	Monday	Tuesday	Wednesday	Thursday	Friday	Saturday

Calendar Activities for February

Classroom Calendar Setup

The use of the calendar in the classroom can provide children with daily practice on learning days, weeks, months, and years. As you plan the setup for your classroom, include enough wall space to staple a calendar grid labeled with the days of the week. Leave space above the grid for the name of the month and the year. Next to the calendar, staple twelve cards labeled with the months of the year and the number of days in each month. (Use the calendar day pattern on page 96.) Leave these items on the wall all year. At the beginning of each month, start with the blank calendar grid. Do not staple anything on the grid that refers to the new month. Leave the days of the week and the year in place.

Introducing the Month of February

Gather all of the items that will go on the calendar for February. You may want to include the name of the month card, number cards, name cards for children who have February birthdays, and picture cards that tell about special February holidays or school events. You may also wish to wrap small treats such as sugarless gum to tape on February birthday dates. Add a special pointer that can be used each day while doing calendar activities. See page 9 for directions on how to make a pointer. Place these items in a picnic basket. Select a puppet that remains in the basket and that you will use only to bring items for each new month. A dog puppet works well because its large mouth can be easily used to grasp each item.

Place the picnic basket in front of the class. Introduce the puppet to children if it is the first time they have seen it or ask them if they remember why the puppet is here. If this is the first time children are seeing it, explain that the puppet will visit on the first day of each month to bring the new calendar items. Then have the puppet pull out the card that has the name of the month. According to the abilities of children, have them name the first letter, count the letters, or find the vowels in the name of the month. Staple the name of the month above the calendar. Have the puppet pull out the new pointer for the teacher or the daily helper to use each day during calendar time.

Next, pull out the number cards for February. You may use plain number cards, or you may want to use seasonal die-cut shapes. By using two or three die-cut shapes, you can incorporate building patterns as part of your daily calendar routine. (See "Developing a Pattern" on page 9.) Place the number one card or die-cut under the day of the week on which February begins. Locate the February name card from the month cards that are stapled next to your calendar. Have children tell how many days this month will have and then count that many spaces on the calendar to indicate the end of the month. You may wish to place a small stop sign as a visual reminder of the end of the month. Save the remaining number cards or die-cut shapes and add one each day.

If there are any children in the class with February birthdays, have the puppet pull the cards out of the basket that have a birthday symbol with the child's name and birth date written on it. Count from the number 1 to find where to staple this as a visual reminder of each child's birthday. If you have included a wrapped treat for each child, tape it on the calendar on the correct day.

Finally, have the puppet bring out cards that have pictures of holidays or special happenings, such as field trips, picture day, or story time in the library. Staple the picture cards on the correct day on the calendar grid. You can use these to practice counting how many days there are until a field trip, a birthday, or a holiday. When the basket is empty, say goodbye to the puppet and return it to the picnic basket. Put the basket away until the next month. Children will look forward to the beginning of each month in order to see what items the puppet will bring for the class calendar.

Making a Heart Pointer

To make a pointer, you will need two 3" heart shapes cut from poster board, a medium-sized dowel rod that is 18" long, and several 12" lengths of narrow red, pink, and white ribbon. Hot-glue the ribbons to the end of the dowel rod so that they lay against the rod. Then hot-glue the two heart shapes to the end of the dowel rod so that the heart shapes cover the glued ends of the ribbons. You may wish to glue glitter on the heart as well. The teacher or daily helper can use this to point to the day of the week, the number, the month, and the year as the class says the date each day.

Developing a Pattern

Practice patterning by writing the numbers 1–28 (29 in a leap year) on red, pink, and white heart shapes, in that order. On the back of all the red hearts, write "I," and on the back of all white hearts, write "U." Leave all the pink hearts blank. For the month of February, place all hearts on the calendar at the beginning of the month, making sure that the numbers are showing. After saying the date for the day, the calendar helper will turn the heart over to reveal part of the secret message. The children will soon recognize the message: I♥U. The message will be repeated several times throughout the month.

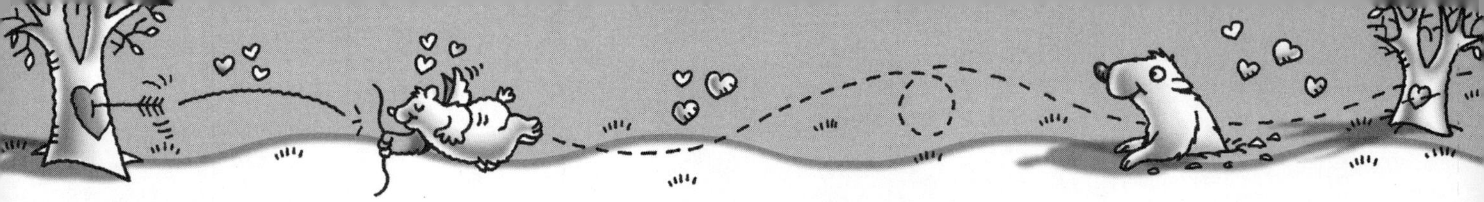

Groundhog Information

Groundhogs are also known as woodchucks.

Groundhogs are rodents that have strong bodies and two sharp front teeth. The groundhog's teeth grow continuously.

Groundhogs have claws that they use to dig in the dirt to make their burrows.

These animals are not only great diggers, but they climb trees and swim, too.

All groundhog burrows are the same: the tunnel begins straight down for about five feet. Then it angles to the side for about ten feet. Finally, the tunnel straightens out. Groundhogs make four or five rooms in their burrows.

The groundhog uses one room specifically as its bathroom. When this room is full, the animal closes the opening with dirt and digs a new room to use as its bathroom.

Groundhogs whistle to alert each other of danger.

Groundhogs love to eat greens, like grass, dandelions, and alfalfa. They also become pests in gardens, eating the vegetables and fruits that people grow.

Groundhogs are true hibernators. They generally hibernate five months in colder climates. In warmer climates, they might be active all year long.

Groundhog Day is February 2. According to folklore, if the groundhog sees its shadow, it is scared and goes back into its burrow for six more weeks. Therefore, there will be six more weeks of winter. If the groundhog does not see its shadow, it knows that it is safe to wake up because there will be an early spring.

Punxsutawney Phil is the most famous groundhog weather forecaster. Each year large crowds visit Phil in Pennsylvania on February 2 to discover his predictions.

Canada has its own version of Punxsutawney Phil. His name is Wiarton Willy.

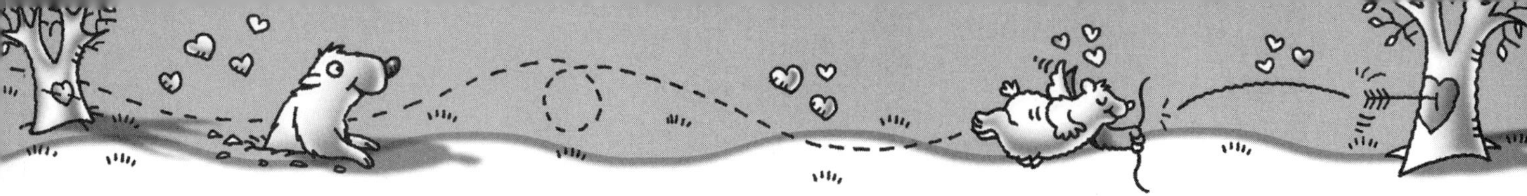

Beanbag Groundhog

Materials

- old, clean socks (preferably brown)
- brown dye (if the socks are white)
- dried beans
- large wiggly eyes
- brown pompoms
- brown and white felt
- fabric glue
- scissors
- yarn
- spoon

Directions

Teacher Preparation: If the socks are white, prepare the dye and process the socks according to the directions on the package. Then cut out pairs of brown ears and white incisor teeth from felt for each child.

1. Spoon beans into the sock until it is half full.
2. Tightly tie and knot the yarn to close the sock.
3. Glue on two eyes, pompom nose, ears, and teeth.
4. Set the "groundhog" aside to dry.

In and Out Groundhog

Materials

- patterns on page 19
- brown paper
- small wiggly eyes
- paper cups
- craft sticks
- markers
- white chalk
- scissors
- glue

Directions

Teacher Preparation: Duplicate the patterns on the brown paper and cut them apart. Provide one groundhog pattern for each child. Cut a slit in the bottom of each cup.

1. Cut out the groundhog.
2. Fold the groundhog on the line.
3. Glue two wiggly eyes on the groundhog.
4. Color a black marker nose and color white chalk teeth.
5. Insert the stick between the folded paper and glue it in place. Set aside to dry.
6. Color the cup with a brown marker.
7. Slide the stick into the cup through the slit.

Groundhog Day Treats

You will need

- chocolate or glazed doughnuts
- oval-shaped cookies
- chocolate chips
- white tube icing
- chocolate syrup (optional, see note below)
- paper plates
- spoons

Note: If using this treat on Groundhog Day or later, you may wish to discover Punxsutawney Phil's forecast. If Phil did not see his shadow, you may wish to omit the use of the chocolate syrup to reinforce the year's prediction.

Directions

1. Squirt dots of icing on one end of a cookie to make the eyes and nose of the groundhog.
2. Place chocolate chips on the icing dots.
3. Squirt two lines of icing below the nose to make the teeth of the groundhog.
4. Place a doughnut on a plate.
5. Push the undecorated end of the cookie into the hole of the doughnut.
6. Use a spoon to drizzle chocolate syrup on the edge of the doughnut to be the groundhog's shadow.

Note: Be aware of children who may have food allergies.

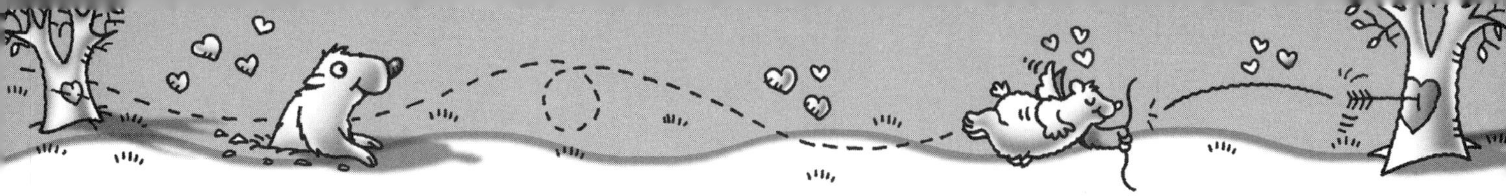

I'm a Little Groundhog

(Sing to the tune of "I'm a Little Teapot.")

Invite children to use the groundhog headbands completed in "Furry Groundhog" on page 16 to wear as they role-play the song. Or have children use the groundhogs made in "In and Out Groundhog" on page 11 to use as they role-play.

I'm a little groundhog, furry and brown,
(Squat.)

Popping up my head and looking around.
(Stand up quickly and look around.)

If I see my shadow, then down I go;
(Point, then squat again.)

Six more weeks of winter—OH, NO!
(Hands touch face.)

Groundhog Poem

Groundhog, groundhog,

What do you say?

Will it be spring,

Or will winter stay?

Burrow In with These Books . . .

Fluffy Meets the Groundhog
by Kate Mullen (Cartwheel Books)

Go to Sleep, Groundhog!
by Judy Cox (Holiday House)

Gregory's Shadow
by Don Freeman (Puffin)

Groundhog Day
by Michelle Aki Becker (Children's Press)

Groundhogs: Woodchucks, Marmots, and Whistle Pigs
by Adele D. Richardson (Bridgestone Books)

It's Groundhog Day
by Steven Kroll (Scholastic)

The Secret of the First One Up
by Iris Hiskey Arno (NorthWord Press)

Signs of the Season

Materials

- pattern on page 20
- white craft paper
- overhead projector
- transparency
- tempera paints
- border or construction paper (optional for border)
- sponge brushes
- large index cards
- crayons
- scissors
- stapler

Directions

Teacher Preparation: Make a transparency of the pattern. Cover the bulletin board with the craft paper. Use the transparency to trace a large groundhog and its burrow in the center of the bulletin board. Paint the groundhog and the burrow. Add a shadow if Punxsutawney Phil sees his shadow on Groundhog Day. Add a festive border or a pattern border made from suns and clouds. Include the poem. Finally, label one side of the board *Winter* and the other side *Spring*. Provide each student with two index cards.

1. Lead children in a discussion of characteristics of both spring and winter. Include the ideas of trees' appearances, emergence of flowers, and animal activities.
2. Draw and color a winter scene on one index card.
3. Draw and color a spring scene on the other index card.
4. Label each drawing *winter* or *spring*.

Have children identify their pictures as winter or spring. Then help them staple the pictures under the correct season label on the bulletin board.

Groundhog Centers

Math Center

Math Standard
Recognizes shapes from different perspectives

Shadow Shape Guess

Materials

- white sheet
- clothesline
- clothespins
- flashlight
- box
- chair
- various familiar objects, such as a block, paintbrush, pair of scissors, pencil, book, etc.

Teacher Preparation: String a clothesline in the center, leaving room for a child to sit. Use clothespins to fasten a sheet to it. Put the chair, flashlight, and the gathered objects in a box on the floor behind the sheet. You may wish to change items in the box during the week.

Invite one child to sit behind the sheet. Have the child choose an item from the box, hold it up next to the sheet, and shine the flashlight behind the object so that the light shines on the sheet. Children in front of the sheet guess the item from the shadow.

Language Center

Language Arts Standard
Recognizes uppercase and lowercase letters

Hurry Home, Groundhog

Materials

- patterns on page 21
- crayons
- scissors
- white construction paper
- file folder
- glue

Teacher Preparation: Duplicate on construction paper, color, and cut out the groundhogs and burrows. Glue the burrows on the inside of a file folder. Write a lowercase letter on each burrow. Write the corresponding capital letters on the groundhogs.

Have children help the groundhogs get back to their burrows by matching the capital letters to the lowercase letters.

Extension: For a phonemic awareness activity, draw or cut out pairs of pictures whose names have the same beginning sounds. For example, cut out magazine pictures of a book and a boat. Glue one picture on a burrow and the other on a groundhog. Children match the groundhog to its burrow by listening for the beginning /b/ sound.

Groundhog Centers

Art Center

Language Arts Standard
Gives feedback, with prompting and support, by sharing and speaking with others

Furry Groundhog

Materials

- pattern on page 22
- stapler
- brushes
- scissors
- white construction paper
- dried coffee grounds
- black marker
- 11" x 18" brown construction paper
- containers
- glue
- spoons

Teacher Preparation: Duplicate the groundhog headband on white paper. Then cut the brown paper into 2-inch x 18-inch strips.

Have children color the eyes and nose of the groundhog black. Invite them to brush glue on the face of the groundhog, leaving the teeth white. Then have children use a spoon to sprinkle the coffee grounds on the glue. Next, have children shake the excess coffee grounds into an empty container. When the glue is dry, have children cut out the faces. Help them staple a brown paper strip to the back, fitting it to their heads. Ask children to describe the texture of their groundhog.

Dramatic Play Center

Language Arts Standard
Uses simple sentences to communicate thoughts and ideas when speaking

Is It Spring?

Materials

- groundhog headbands (completed in "Furry Groundhog" above)
- large box
- flashlight

Invite children to take turns being a groundhog and a shadow maker. Have one child wear his or her groundhog headband and squat in the box. Another child sits behind the box and holds the flashlight. Everyone in the center recites the "Groundhog Poem" from the bulletin board. When the groundhog pops up at the end of the poem, the child holding the flashlight chooses to make a shadow or not. The groundhog tells his or her weather forecast of six more weeks of winter or an early spring based on the shadow.

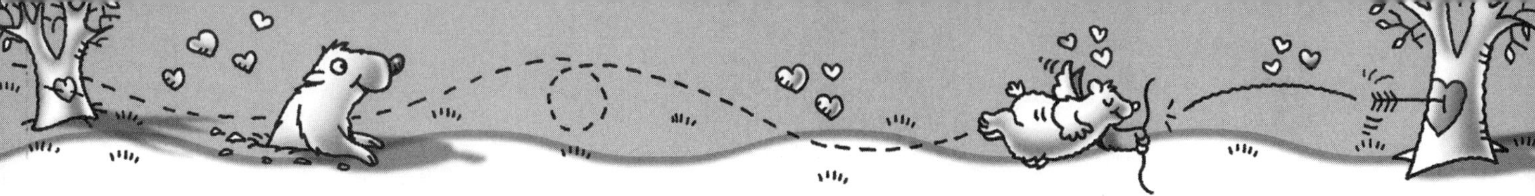

Groundhog Centers

Writing Center

Language Arts Standard
Uses letters to represent words

Where Is the Groundhog?

Materials

- activity masters on pages 23 and 24
- crayons or markers
- pencils
- construction paper
- stapler
- scissors

Teacher Preparation: Duplicate the position booklet pages. Make a cover from construction paper and assemble the books. Provide a copy for each child.

Remind children that groundhogs like to dig, swim, and climb. Then invite children to make a booklet about a groundhog. Read aloud the sentences on the booklet pages as children follow along. Have children trace the position word and draw and color a picture of a groundhog that corresponds to the sentence.

Game Center

Math Standard
Represents data using a tally table

Beanbags and Burrows

Materials

- craft paper
- scrap paper
- markers
- pencils
- groundhog beanbags (completed in "Beanbag Groundhog" on page 11)

Teacher Preparation: Draw a large burrow similar to the one shown on page 23 on craft paper.

Show children how to mark a tally. Then have children write their names on scrap paper. Invite children to take turns tossing their groundhog beanbags on the burrow. Have them mark a tally on their scrap paper for each time the groundhog lands inside a room. The child with the most tallies wins.

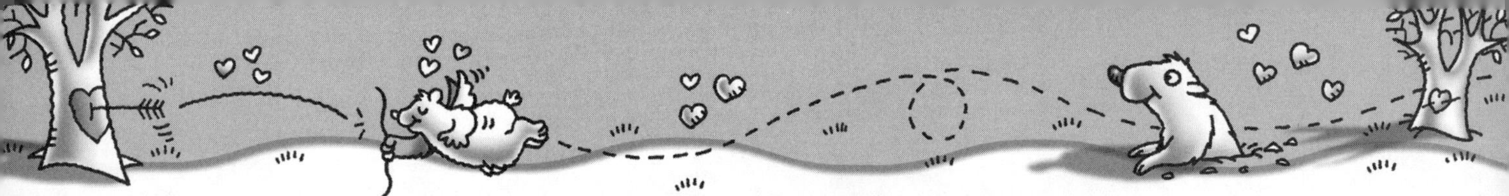

Groundhog Centers

Block Center

Language Arts Standard
Uses simple sentences to communicate thoughts and ideas when speaking

Burrowing in the Blocks

Materials

- groundhog beanbags (completed in "Beanbag Groundhog" on page 11)

Tell children that groundhogs eat lots of food to prepare for their long winter nap and that the animals go in and out of their burrows frequently looking for food in the fall. Then have children use blocks to create a burrow with rooms. Encourage them to pretend that their beanbags are real groundhogs in the fall season. Challenge volunteers to describe the rooms and how their groundhogs are preparing for winter.

Science Center

Science Standard
Observes changes of objects in the sky

Sun and Shadows

Materials

- flashlight
- white craft paper
- markers

Teacher Preparation: Cover about a five-foot wide by five-foot tall wall area with craft paper. Draw a model of Earth in the center about one foot off the floor. Draw a large half circle on the paper, starting at the floor on one side of the paper and ending by the floor on the opposite side. Draw five sun pictures along the line.

Lead children in a discussion, explaining how Earth moves around the sun. Point out that the sun looks like it is at different points depending on where Earth is at that time of day. Talk about how the shadows change with the position of the sun. Then have one child stand in front of Earth. Another child holds the flashlight against the wall at each sun position, shining the light on the child who represents Earth. Have remaining children tell how Earth's shadow changes.

Front and Back Groundhog Patterns

Use with "In and Out Groundhog" on page 11.

Groundhog Pattern

Use with "Signs of the Season" on page 14.

Groundhog, groundhog,
What do you say?
Will it be spring,
Or will winter stay?

Groundhogs and Burrows Patterns

Use with "Hurry Home, Groundhog" on page 15.

Groundhog Headband Pattern

Use with the "I'm a Little Groundhog" song on page 13, "Furry Groundhog" on page 16, and "Is It Spring?" on page 16.

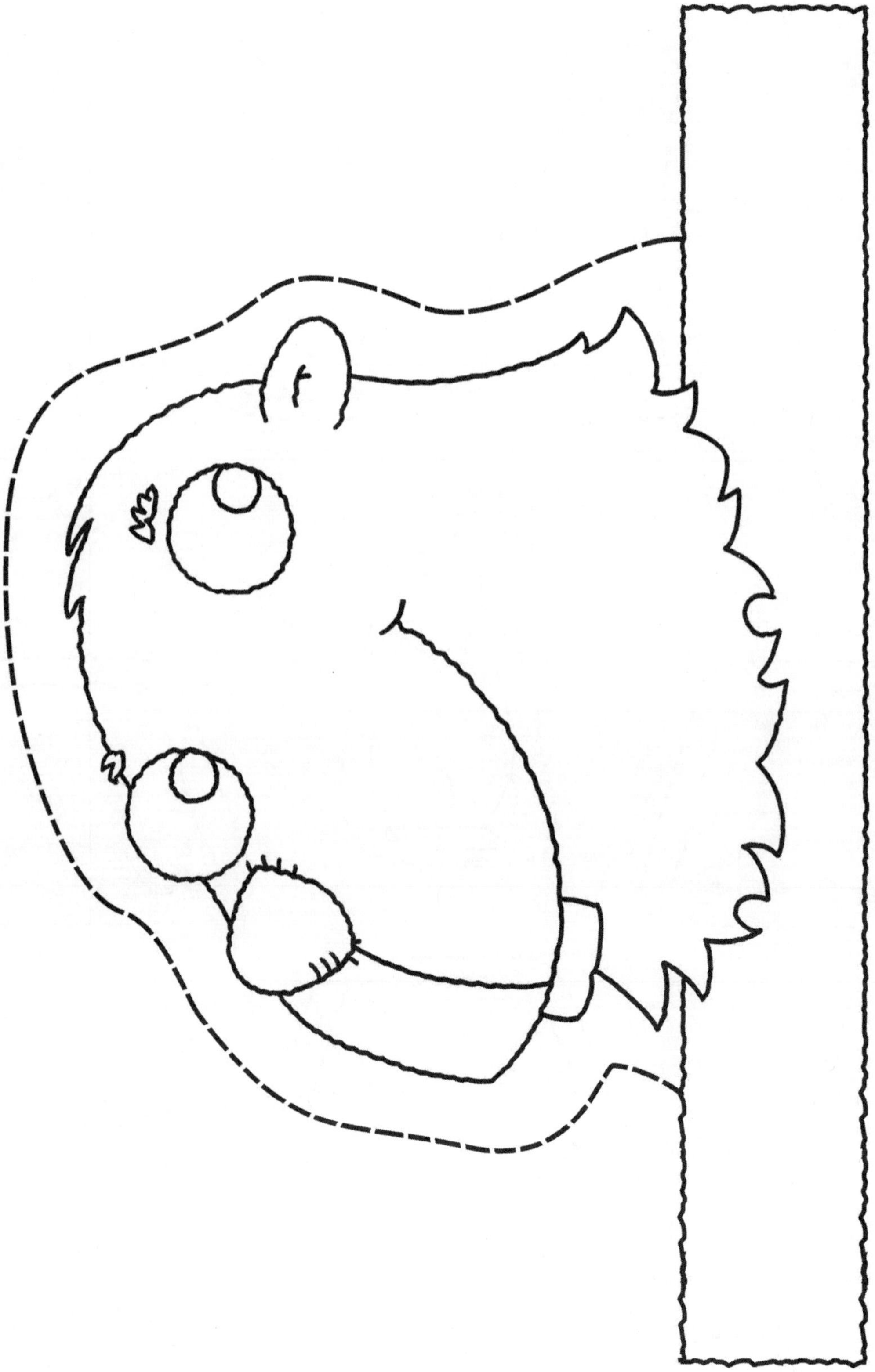

Position Booklet

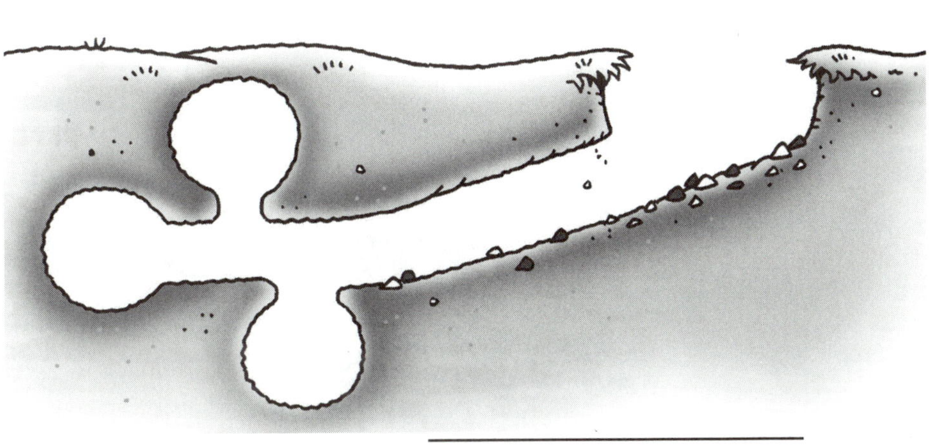

The groundhog is in. 1

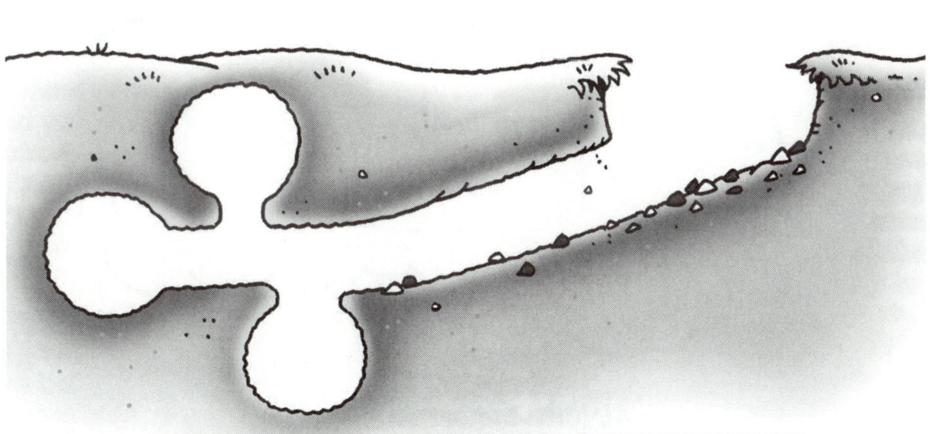

The groundhog is out. 2

Directions: Use with "Where Is the Groundhog?" on page 17. Have children trace the position word and draw and color a groundhog that corresponds to the sentence.

Position Booklet

The groundhog is in.

3

The groundhog is out.

4

Directions: Use with "Where Is the Groundhog?" on page 17. Have children trace the position word and draw and color a groundhog that corresponds to the sentence.

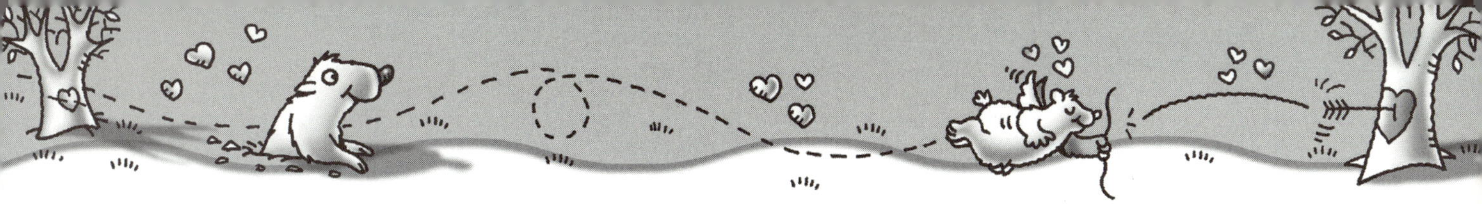

Talking from the Heart

The origin of Valentine's Day began during ancient times in the spring. Single women put their names into a vase. Single men would choose a name to find a sweetheart. The men would wear those names on their sleeves. The saying "to wear your heart on your sleeve" came from this practice. The phrase now means that it is easy for other people to know how you are feeling.

Valentine's Day was named for the Roman priest Valentine. An emperor said that no soldier could marry because having a family was a distraction. Valentine defied the ruler and married young soldiers and their sweethearts anyway. Valentine was put to death on February 14 for disobeying the emperor.

The early Catholic church made Valentine a saint. They declared that February 14 would be a day to remember all saints, but people only remembered the story of Valentine.

The heart was believed to be the center of all emotions long ago. It became a symbol of love because a person "gave their whole heart" to another when falling in love.

Cupid was the prankster son of Venus, the goddess of love. He shot magical arrows to make people fall in love. The person hit with one of Cupid's arrows would fall in love with the first person he or she saw.

An *X* became associated with a kiss based on traditions in medieval times. Many people could not write. They would draw an *X* in front of a witness and then kiss the mark to show that the mark was sincerely made.

Red roses have several significant meanings for Valentine's Day. It was the favorite flower of Venus, the goddess of love. Moreover, in the language of flowers, a rose means love.

Lace became a popular symbol because of another tradition. Women often carried handkerchiefs made of lace. When a woman dropped her handkerchief, a man would retrieve it. Some women dropped their handkerchiefs to get a man's attention or to encourage his romantic interest.

Lovebirds became a symbol of the holiday because people believed that birds found their mates by February 14. Also, it was believed that lovebirds mated for life and could not live when their mates died. Finally, lovebirds sit closely together, like sweethearts.

Valentine Cardholder

Materials

- plastic plates
- red, white, and pink yarn
- red, white, and pink construction paper
- permanent marker
- different sizes of heart patterns (optional)
- doilies
- art supplies (sequins, glitter, yarn, ribbon)
- hole punch
- glue
- scissors
- stapler

Directions

Teacher Preparation: Cut plates in half. Provide each child with 1½ plates. Place a half plate over a whole plate. Staple the plates together in three places on the half plate. Hole punch the outer rim of the whole plate at one-inch intervals. Cut different colors of yarn into two-yard lengths. You may wish to provide a variety of sizes and colors of heart patterns on construction paper.

1. Starting at the top, thread yarn through a hole. Leave about a foot of yarn hanging free to use to tie a bow.
2. Use the yarn to sew the plates together.
3. Tie the ends of the yarn to make a bow.
4. Cut out different sizes and colors of hearts.
5. Use the art supplies to decorate the cardholder.
6. Write a name on the rim along the bottom.

Cupid's Arrows and Quiver

Materials

- patterns on page 34
- craft sticks
- tall paper cups
- red, white, and pink construction paper
- scissors
- glue
- red markers

Directions

Teacher Preparation: Duplicate the patterns on the different colors of construction paper. Cut them apart.

1. Get four craft sticks. Write your name on one side of each stick.
2. Cut out and glue two small hearts on one end of a stick, being careful to make sure that the edges align. The heart points are pointing away from the stick.
3. Cut out and glue two large hearts on the other end of the stick, being careful to make sure that the edges align. The heartpoints are pointing the same way as the small hearts.
4. Make three more "arrows." Set all the arrows aside to dry.
5. Glue a Cupid and other hearts to the cup to make a quiver for the arrows.
6. Put the dry arrows in Cupid's quiver.

Extension: Invite children to play a game. Have them hold the cups with the toes of their shoes while standing. Have children try to drop all four arrows into the cups.

Queen of Heart Tarts

You will need

- prepared pie crust
- strawberry jam
- strawberries
- large heart cookie cutter
- baking trays
- pancake turner
- paper plates
- craft sticks
- knife

Directions

Teacher Preparation: Slice the strawberries. Use the slices that look like hearts.

1. Unfold the pie crust and cut heart shapes with the cookie cutter.
2. Place the hearts on a baking tray.
3. Bake the dough according to the package.
4. Put each heart on a plate to cool.
5. Spread jam on the hearts.
6. Top with a heart-shaped strawberry.

Note: Be aware of children who may have food allergies.

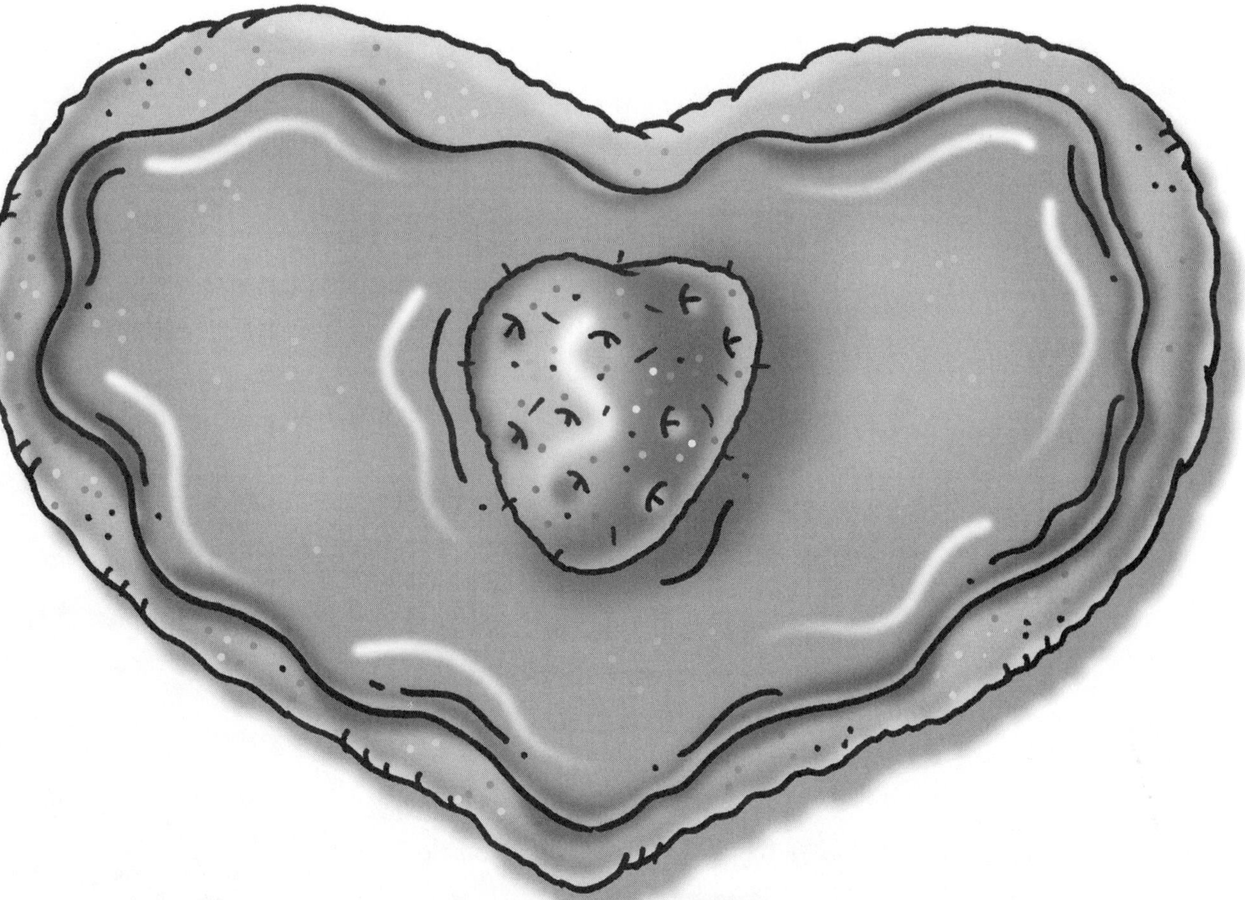

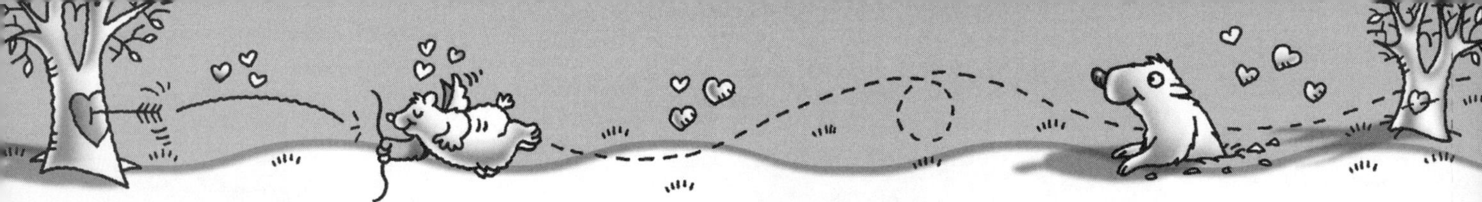

Five Little Valentines

Five little valentines were having a race.
The first little valentine was frilly with lace.
The second little valentine had a funny face.
The third little valentine said, "I love you!"
The fourth little valentine said, "I do, too."
The fifth little valentine was sly as a fox.
He ran the fastest to the valentine box.

Books to Love

Arthur's Valentine
by Marc Brown (Little, Brown & Company)

Counting Kisses: A Kiss and Read Book
by Karen Katz (Little Simon)

The Day It Rained Hearts
by Felicia Bond (Laura Geringer)

Henry and Mudge and Mrs. Hopper's House
by Cynthia Rylant (Simon & Schuster Children's Publishing)

Roses Are Pink, Your Feet Really Stink
by Diane deGroat (HarperTrophy)

The Valentine Bears
by Jan Brett (Clarion Books)

Valentine's Day
by Gail Gibbons (Holiday House)

The Very Special Valentine
by Maggie Kneen (Chronicle Books)

Love Bug Hugs

Materials

- pattern on page 35
- white craft paper
- overhead projector
- transparency
- tempera paints
- stapler
- sponge brushes
- tag board
- pipe cleaners
- scissors
- glue
- heart-shaped sequins or very small stickers
- art supplies (sequins, glitter, yarn, ribbon)
- red, white, and pink construction paper

Directions

Teacher Preparation: Write or type the poem about the same size as it appears on the pattern and make multiple copies. Cut the poems apart. Make a transparency of the love bugs. Cover the board with the craft paper. Use the transparency to trace the enlarged love bugs in the center of the bulletin board. Paint the bugs with red, white, and pink paints. Cut out 6-inch hearts and write the children's names on them. Staple the hearts to make a color-pattern border. Include the poem if you wish. Cut out large and small half-heart shapes from the tag board for body and head patterns. Provide each child with a large and small pattern. Cut the construction paper into squares that are about the same size as the patterns when folded. Cut pipe cleaners into four long equal pieces and others into two short equal pieces. Each child will need two short and four long pieces.

1. Fold a large square of construction paper in half.
2. Lay the large half-heart pattern on the paper, matching the straight edges.
3. Trace the pattern to make the body of the bug.
4. Repeat steps 1 through 3 using a small heart to make the head of the bug.
5. Cut out both hearts.
6. Glue the two hearts together so that the points overlap.
7. Glue two short pipe cleaners to the head to make antennae.
8. Glue a sequin or attach a sticker on each antennae.
9. Glue four long pipe cleaners to the body to make legs and arms.
10. Decorate the "love bug" with the art supplies.
11. Glue a copy of the poem to the backside of the bug.

Have children find their names in the border and identify the color pattern. Then staple their love bugs to the bulletin board.

Valentine Centers

Math Center

Math Standard
Compares and orders objects to some attribute

Hoppin' Hearts

Materials

- craft paper
- red tempera paint
- masking tape

Teacher Preparation: Paint six hearts in different sizes on the craft paper. Hearts should be close enough that children can safely jump to each one no matter on which heart they stand.

Invite children to take turns hopping to the hearts in order from the smallest to the largest or from the largest to the smallest.

Dramatic Play Center

Language Arts Standard
Writes labels

Stamp and Deliver

Materials

- heart stamp
- ink pad
- writing tools
- mail pouches
- mail carrier hats
- balance scale
- recycled envelopes (collected from bulk mailings)

Teacher Preparation: Set up a post office in the dramatic play center.

Invite children to dress the part of postal workers and mail carriers when they bring in their valentines. Make sure that each child writes the name of the person the valentine is going to and the name of the person it is from. They can "mail" valentines by stamping a heart stamp and delivering them to the "mailbox" cardholders completed in "Valentine Card Holder" on page 26.

Valentine Centers

Language Center

Language Arts Standard
Recognizes rhyming words

Valentine Rhyme Time

Materials

- activity master on page 36
- crayons
- copying paper

Teacher Preparation: Provide each child with a copy of the activity master.

Have children draw lines to match pictures whose names rhyme.

Art Center

Math Standard
Counts with understanding

Heart Sun Catchers

Materials

- wax paper
- permanent marker
- scissors
- red, white, and pink tissue paper
- art supplies (sequins, glitter, yarn, ribbon)
- red, white, or pink yarn
- containers
- hole punch
- liquid starch
- paintbrushes
- wet paper towels

Teacher Preparation: Trace 8-inch hearts on the wax paper using the permanent marker. Cut tissue paper into 1-inch x 2-inch rectangles.

Have children dip the tissue paper rectangles in the starch and lay them inside the wax paper heart. Tell them to overlap the edges of the tissue paper. When the heart is fully covered with tissue paper, have children brush a thin layer of starch over the heart. Invite them to press different art supplies on the heart to decorate it. When the heart is dry, cut it out. Punch a hole in the heart and hang it with yarn in front of a window.

Challenge children to count how many different kinds of art supplies they used to make their sun catchers.

Valentine Centers

Puzzle Center

Math Standard
Applies and adapts a variety of appropriate strategies to solve problems

Broken Hearts

Materials

- patterns on page 39
- scissors
- red, white, and pink poster board

Teacher Preparation: Enlarge each heart puzzle pattern. Trace each heart on the poster board and cut it into puzzle pieces.

Have children piece the heart puzzles together.

Science Center

Science Standard
Understands characteristics of organisms

Heartbeat Speed

Materials

- pattern on page 37
- activity master on page 38
- books that show a human heart
- ball
- crayons
- jump rope
- clock with second hand

Teacher Preparation: Duplicate and laminate one copy of the human heart pattern. Then duplicate the activity master.

Tell children that the heart moves blood throughout the body. The heartbeat is made as parts of the heart open and close. Then help children find their heartbeat on their arms or necks. Have children look at the picture of the human heart in the center and discuss how it is the same as and different from the valentine heart symbol. Explain how to time one minute with a second hand on a watch or clock. Challenge children to do each activity on the chart for one minute to see if their hearts slow down or speed up. Have them feel their heartbeats. Children color the blue crayons if their heartbeats slow down. They color the red crayons if their heartbeats speed up.

Valentine Centers

Writing Center

Language Arts Standard
Recognizes uppercase and lowercase letters

Love Bug Partners

Materials

- paper
- pencils
- love bugs (completed in "Love Bug Hugs" on page 29)

Tell children that the love bugs will be taken off the bulletin board so they can share them with someone who needs a hug. Then invite children to dictate a sentence telling to whom they would give their love bug and why the person needs a hug.

Have children trace the letters in each word in their sentence. Encourage children to identify the uppercase and lowercase letters in their sentence.

Sensory Center

Math Standard
Identifies, reproduces, creates, and describes simple patterns

Heart Patterns

Materials

- sand table
- spray bottle
- heart cookie cutters (variety of sizes)

Teacher Preparation: Use a spray bottle to keep the sand damp so the patterns will show up clearly.

Invite partners to take turns making patterns in the sand using the cookie cutters. One child makes a pattern by pressing the cutters into the sand while the partner faces away. Then the partner looks at the pattern, describes it aloud, and reproduces it.

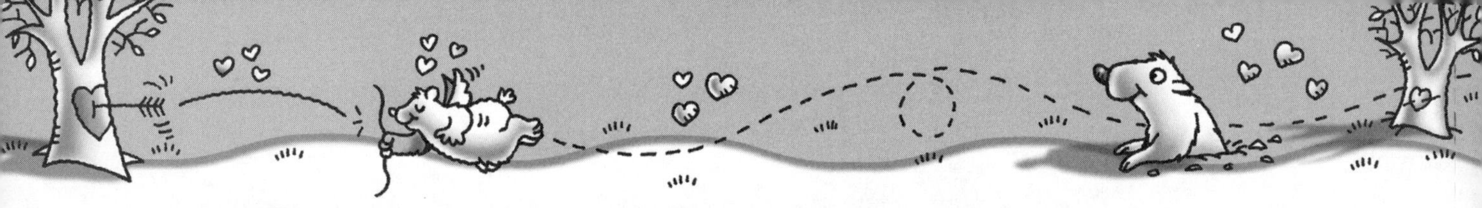

Cupids and Hearts Patterns

Use with "Cupid's Arrows and Quiver" on page 26.

Love Bug Patterns

Use with "Love Bug Hugs" on page 29.

I'm a little love bug
That came to visit you.
I'm here to give you a big hug
And make you smile, too.

Name ______________________________

Valentine Rhyme Time

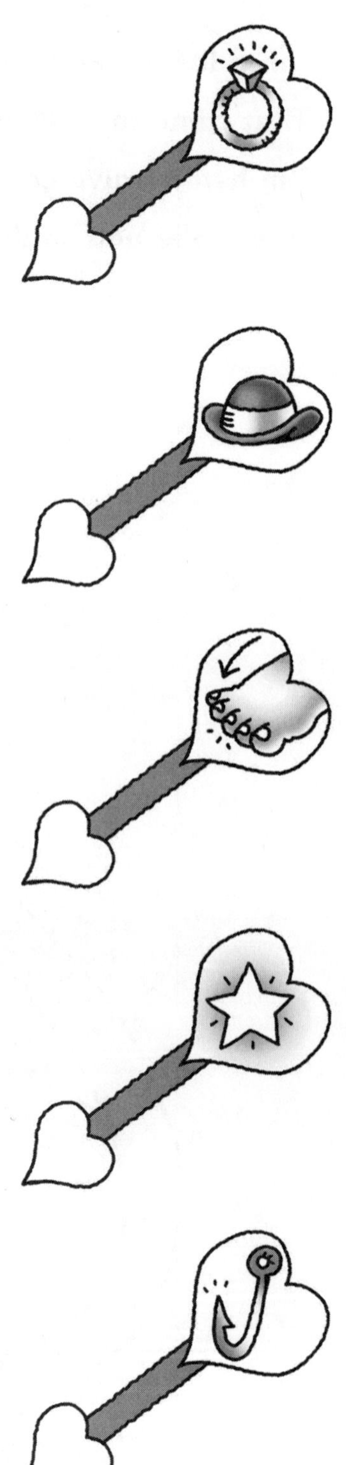

Directions: Use with "Valentine Rhyme Time" on page 31. Have children draw lines to match pictures whose names rhyme.

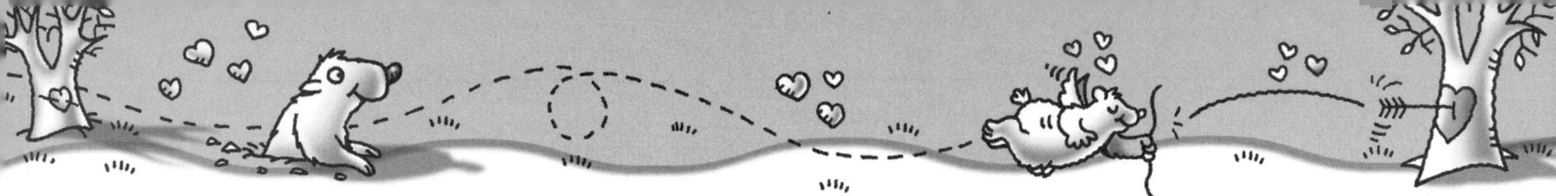

Human Heart Pattern

Use with "Heartbeat Speed" on page 32.

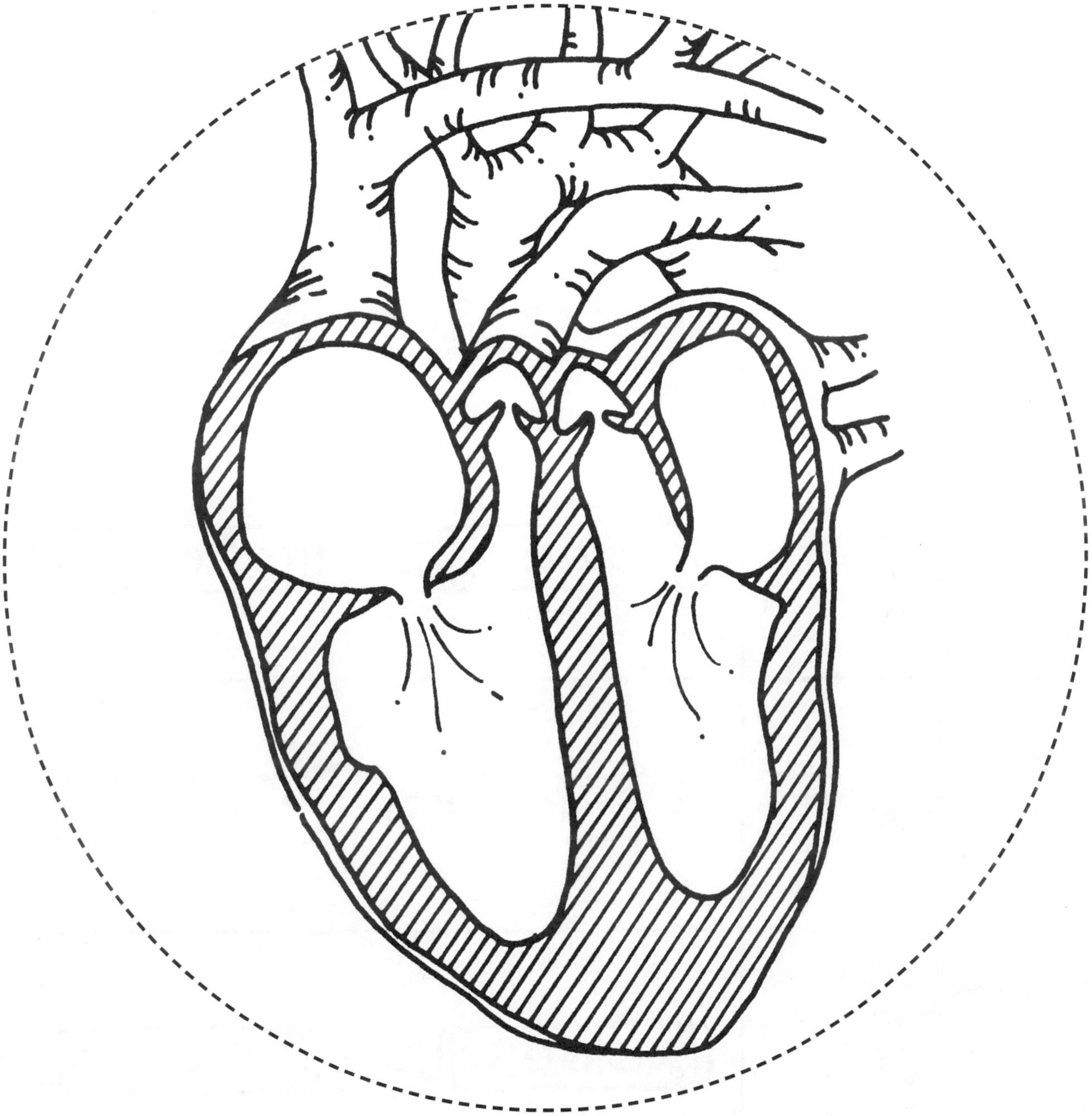

Name ______________________

Get Moving

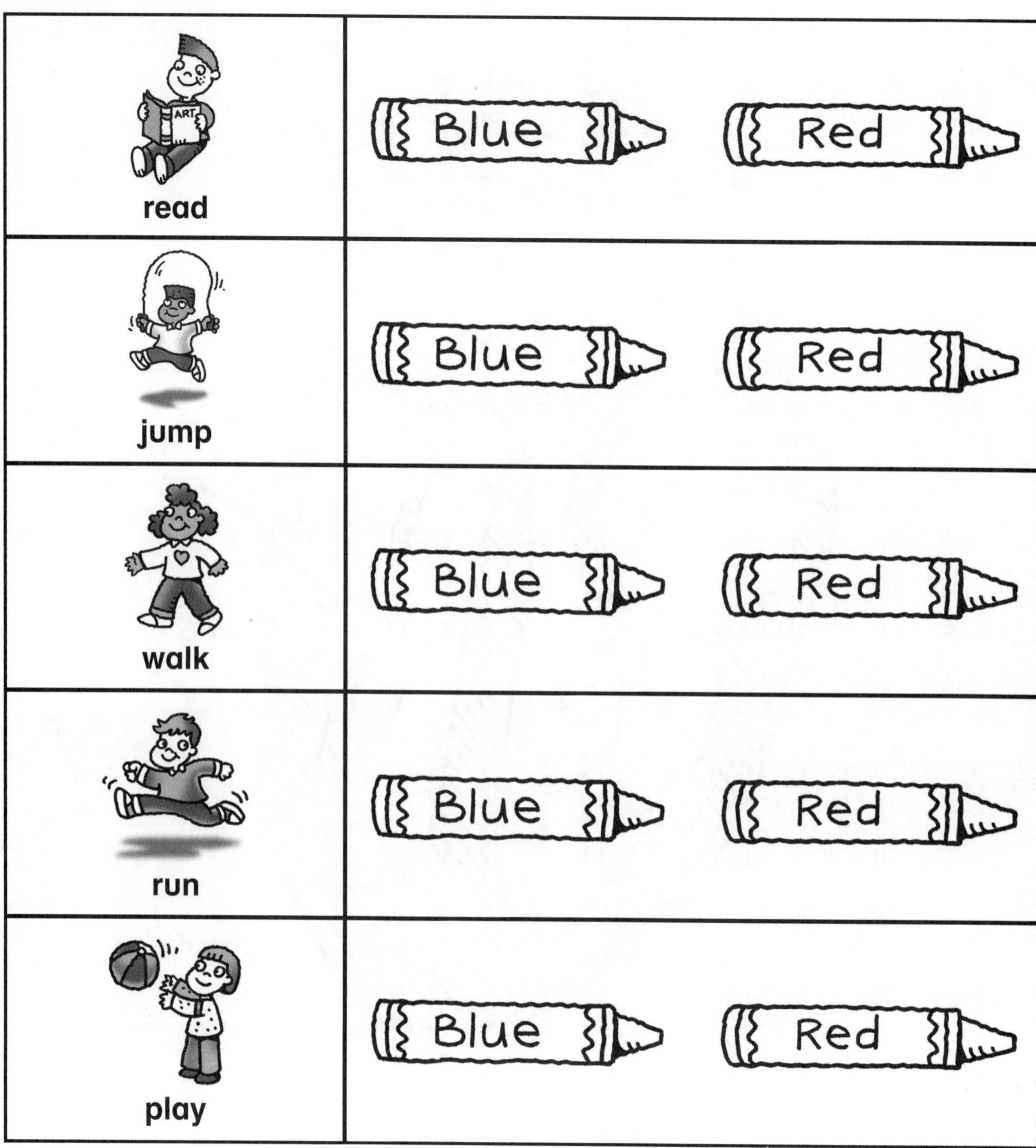

Directions: Use with "Heartbeat Speed" on page 32. Have children do each activity on the chart for one minute to see if their hearts slow down or speed up. Have them check their heartbeats. Children color the blue crayon if their heartbeats slow down. They color the red crayon if their heartbeats speed up.

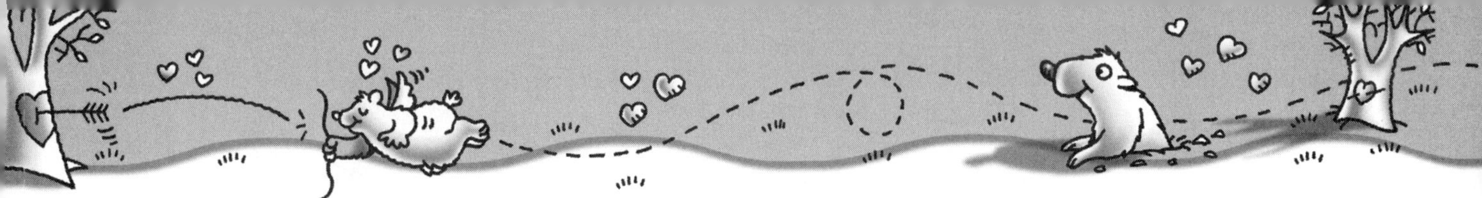

Heart Puzzles Patterns

Use with "Broken Hearts" on page 32.

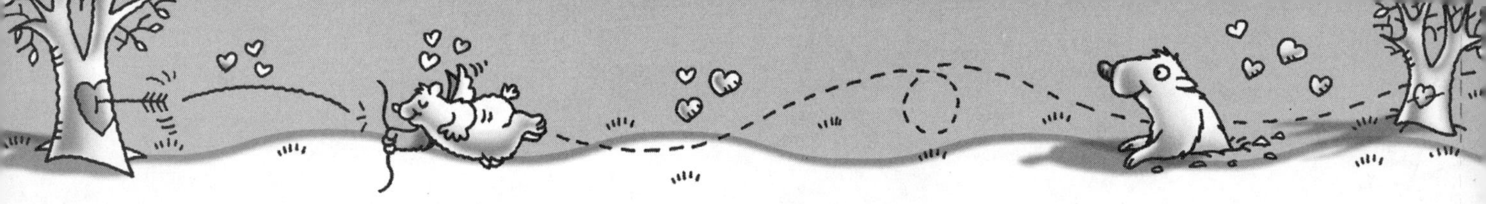

Information Worth Biting Into

A dentist and a dental hygienist take care of teeth. They look at the teeth, gums, and other parts of the mouth to make sure the mouth is healthy.

Different teeth have different jobs. Some teeth are long and flat. These teeth are good for biting. Some teeth are sharp. These teeth are good for tearing. Some teeth are big and flat on the top. These teeth are good for chewing.

The first dental floss was made from silk.

If children brush with fluoride toothpaste, they will have about 24 percent fewer cavities.

People who drink at least three sodas a day generally have 62 percent greater chance of getting cavities and other dental problems.

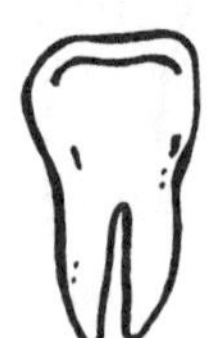

Dentists suggest that people brush between two and three minutes each time; however, most people only brush 45 to 70 seconds at a time.

Adults have 32 teeth. Most children who are between the ages of three and five have 20 teeth. These teeth are baby teeth.

The hard, white part of the tooth is the enamel. Dentin is under the enamel. It is a soft material filled with holes. The layer inside the dentin is called the pulp. It is filled with nerves and blood vessels.

Plaque is a film of bacteria and mucus that covers teeth. It makes acids that cause tooth decay and gum disease. Plaque that stays on the teeth can harden. Hardened plaque is called tartar.

To floss your teeth, wrap floss around two fingers and slide it between the teeth. Curve the floss around each tooth as you move it up and down.

A Toothy Grin

Materials

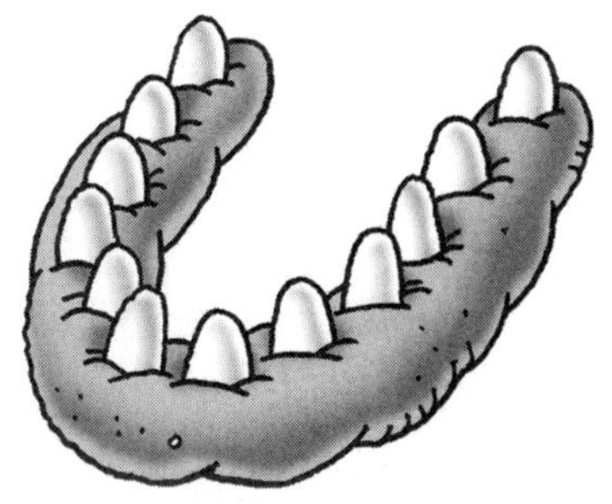

- 1 cup flour
- ½ cup salt
- 1 cup water
- 1 tablespoon cooking oil
- 2 teaspoons cream of tartar
- instant strawberry drink mix
- navy beans
- wax paper
- self-sealing plastic bags
- small paper plates
- mirror

Directions

Teacher Preparation: Make the salt dough in advance. Each child will need about ⅓ cup of dough. In a saucepan, mix the flour, salt, water, oil, cream of tartar, and drink mix. Cook the mixture over heat for three minutes, stirring occasionally. When the mixture forms a ball, remove the pan from the heat and cool it on wax paper. Knead the dough when totally cool. Store the dough in a plastic bag.

1. Look in a mirror to count the bottom teeth.
2. Roll the dough into a 6-inch snake.
3. Form a U-shape with the dough and set it on a plate.
4. Count out the same number of beans as the bottom teeth.
5. Push the beans into the dough so they are upright and look like teeth.
6. Set aside to dry for several days.

Tooth Puppet

Materials

- patterns on page 49
- small paper plates
- tempera paint
- white, black, tan, and pink construction paper
- mini-marshmallows
- paintbrushes
- paint containers
- glue
- scissors

Directions

Teacher Preparation: Duplicate, trace, and cut out the patterns for each child: two white eyes, two black pupils, one tan nose, and one pink tongue.

1. Fold a plate in half.
2. Paint the inside of the plate red.
3. Glue the eyes and nose on one side of the folded plate.
4. Glue the tongue on the inside of the plate.
5. Glue the marshmallows along the inside top and bottom rims of the plate for teeth.
6. Set the puppet aside to dry.

Apple Slice Smile

You will need

- large red apples
- creamy peanut butter or cream cheese
- mini-marshmallows
- paper plates
- craft sticks
- knife

Directions

Teacher Preparation: Cut each apple into eight slices. Remove the seeds and core. Each child will need two apple slices and one plate.

1. Spread peanut butter or cream cheese on one side of each apple slice.
2. Press 6 to 8 marshmallows, flat side up, into one apple. Make sure the marshmallows are near the edge closest to the apple skin.
3. Set the other apple, peanut butter or cream cheese side down, on the marshmallows.

Note: Be aware of children who may have food allergies.

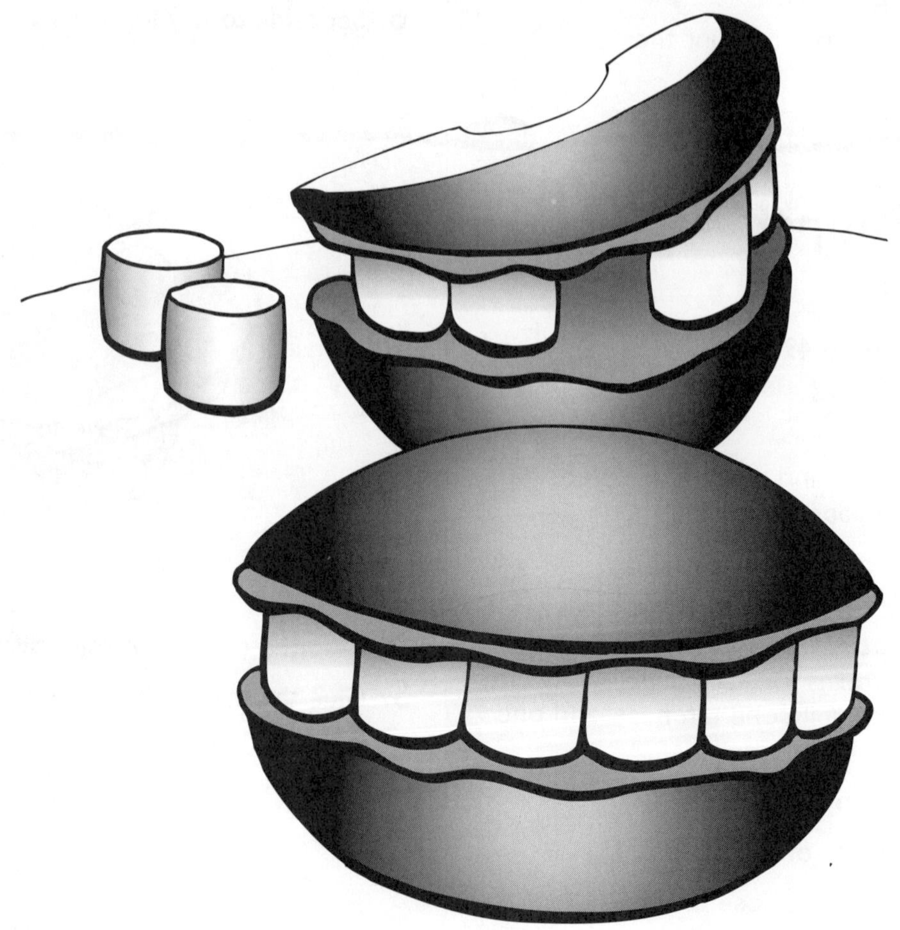

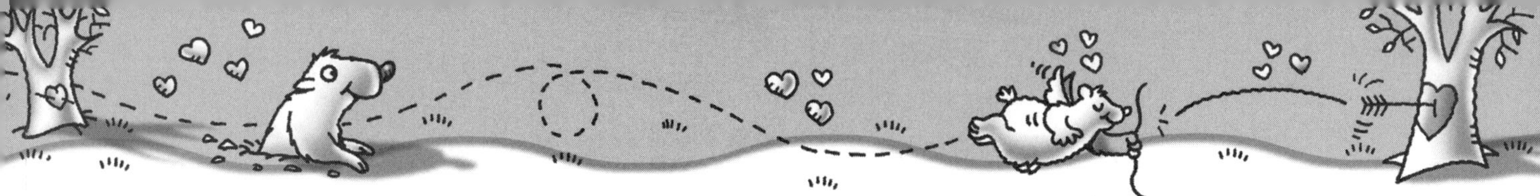

Brush, Brush, Brush Your Teeth

(Sing to the tune of "Row, Row, Row Your Boat.")

Brush, brush, brush your teeth.
Brush them every day.
Using toothpaste on your brush
Will help stop tooth decay!

Floss, floss, floss your teeth.
Floss them every day.
Using string to clean between
Will help stop tooth decay!

Clean, clean, clean your teeth.
Clean them every day.
If you brush and floss your teeth,
Then you'll help stop tooth decay!

Take a Bite out of These Books. . .

Arthur's Tooth
by Marc Brown (Little, Brown & Company)

Brush Well: A Look at Dental Care
by Katie Bagley (Brookstone Books)

Brush Your Teeth Please
by Leslie McGuire (Reader's Digest)

Dragon Teeth and Parrot Beaks: Even Creatures Brush Their Teeth
by Almute Grohmann (Edition Q)

How Many Teeth?
by Paul Showers (HarperCollins)

Rotten Teeth
by Laura Simms (Houghton Mifflin Company)

Throw Your Tooth on the Roof: Tooth Traditions from Around the World
by Selby Beeler (Houghton Mifflin)

Tooth Fairy
by Audrey Wood
(Child's Play International Limited)

Brush Up on Your Smile

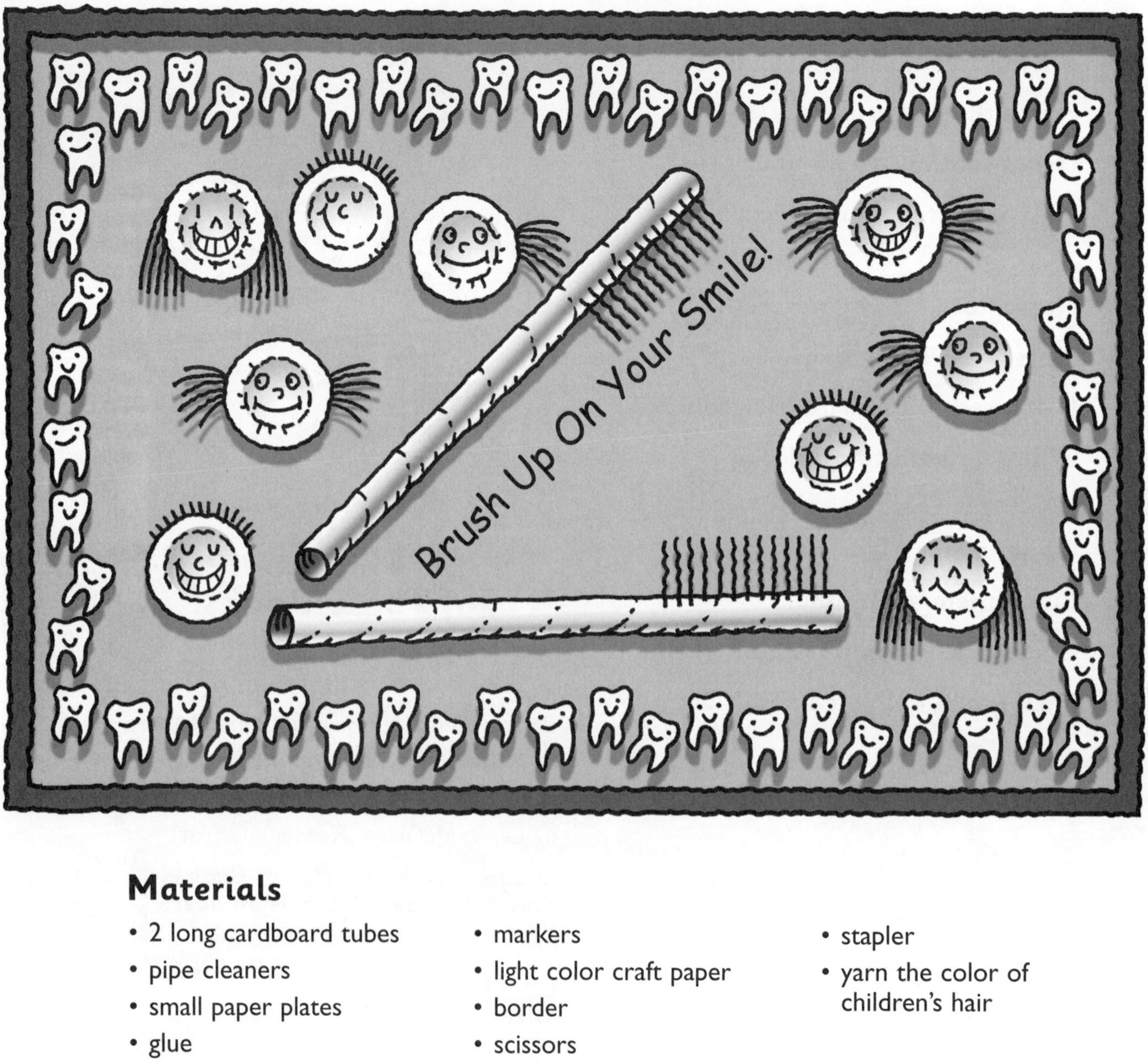

Materials

- 2 long cardboard tubes
- pipe cleaners
- small paper plates
- glue
- markers
- light color craft paper
- border
- scissors
- stapler
- yarn the color of children's hair

Directions

Teacher Preparation: Cover the board with the craft paper. Poke small holes in one end of each tube to make rows for the toothbrush bristles. Cut pipe cleaners in half. Put a drop of glue on one end of the pipe cleaners and insert them in the holes. Staple the "brushes" to the board. Add a festive border and caption.

1. Draw a face on the paper plate. Include a big smile with teeth showing.
2. Glue yarn on the plate for hair.

Staple the paper plate faces on the bulletin board.

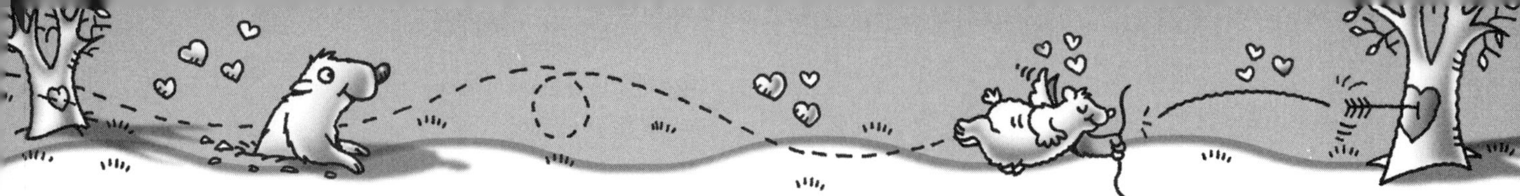

Healthy Teeth Centers

Language Center

Language Arts Standard
Knows the alphabetical order of letters

The ABC's of Teeth

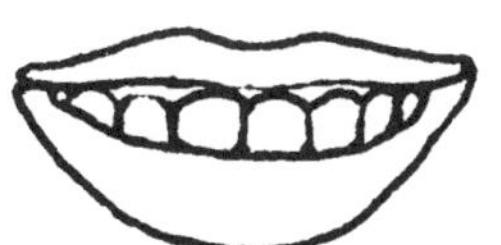

Materials

- activity master on page 50
- crayons

Teacher Preparation: Duplicate the activity master.

Invite children to write the missing letters.

Math Center

Math Standard
Connects numerals to the quantities they represent

Tooth Count

Materials

- activity master on page 51
- scissors
- glue
- crayons

Teacher Preparation: Duplicate the activity master.

Have children cut out the teeth and glue them in the smile with the corresponding number. Children may wish to color the page.

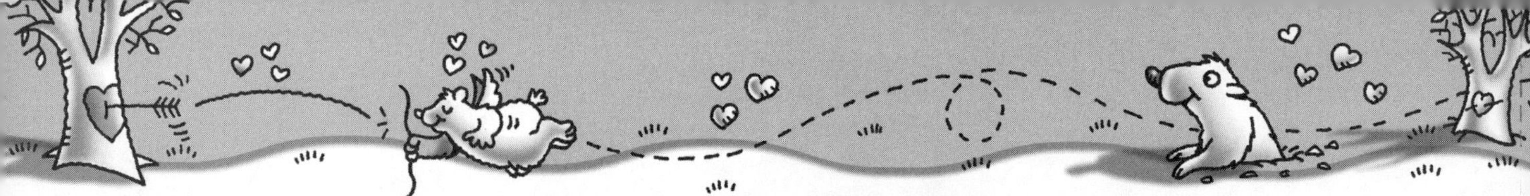

Healthy Teeth Centers

Sensory Center

Language Arts Standard
Uses simple sentences to communicate thoughts and ideas when speaking

What's Missing?

Materials

- old dental tools
- navy beans
- toothbrush
- tub
- toothpaste

Teacher Preparation: Obtain old tools by asking local dentists for discarded tools. Fill the tub with navy beans.

Display and identify how each tool is used. Invite one child to hide a tool while the others turn away from the tub. Once the center members face the tub, children take turns guessing which tool is missing. The correct guesser searches for the tool in the tub and pulls it out.

Challenge volunteers to explain how they determined which tool was missing.

Science Center

Science Standard
Understands science and technology

X-ray Play

Materials

- tooth x-ray
- white paint
- black construction paper
- clean meat trays
- sponges
- water
- scissors

Teacher Preparation: Cut sponges into tooth shapes with roots similar to those on the x-ray. Mix the paint with water to thin it.

Display a tooth x-ray. Challenge children to investigate what it does and how it helps people. Have children dip the sponges into the paint and make x-ray prints on the paper.

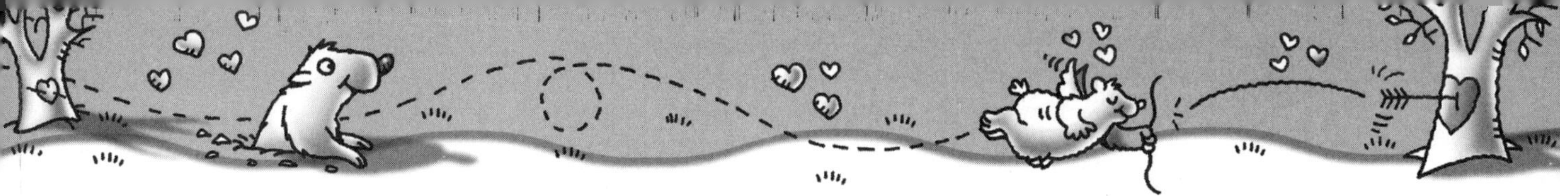

Healthy Teeth Centers

Writing Center

Language Arts Standard
Uses letters to represent words

Tooth Talk

Materials

- activity master on page 52
- crayons

Teacher Preparation: Duplicate the activity master to provide one for each child.

Invite children to draw facial features on the tooth. Then ask them to write or dictate a sentence telling what advice their tooth would tell everyone about taking good care of their teeth.

Art Center

Language Arts Standard
Writes own name correctly and legibly

Brushing Up

Materials

- toothbrushes
- easel paper
- containers
- easels
- tempera paint

Teacher Preparation: Pour paint into separate containers.

Have children paint with toothbrushes. They can use the toothbrushes to draw with, make prints, or flick with a finger. Have children write their names on their own paintings.

Healthy Teeth Centers

Game Center

Math Standard
Connects numerals to the quantities they represent

Visit the Dentist

Materials

- activity master on page 51
- markers or crayons
- patterns on pages 53 and 54
- glue
- poster board (optional)
- file folder
- color counters
- scissors

Teacher Preparation: Duplicate the activity master several times. Color the smiles, cut out the teeth, and glue the teeth to the appropriate smile. Cut the smiles apart to make game cards. You may wish to glue them to poster board to make the cards sturdier. Next, duplicate the board game patterns and color each section. Glue both parts of the board to a file folder and laminate.

Have children shuffle the smile cards and turn them facedown. Children take turns picking the top card and moving that number of spaces. The first child to get to the dentist wins.

Dramatic Play Center

Language Arts Standard
Uses information from what they have learned to develop vocabulary

Egg-stra Good Dental Care

Materials

- hard-boiled eggs
- cola soda
- floss
- egg cartons
- toothbrush
- dental coats or big, white shirts
- plastic cups
- toothpaste

Teacher Preparation: Let the eggs soak in cups of cola overnight.

Invite children to role-play dentists. Have them floss the "teeth" on upturned egg cartons. Then have them brush the "plaque" off the egg "patient" with a toothbrush and toothpaste. Ask children to explain to the patient how to brush and floss properly, as well as the importance of tooth care.

Tooth Puppet Patterns

Use with "Tooth Puppet" on page 41.

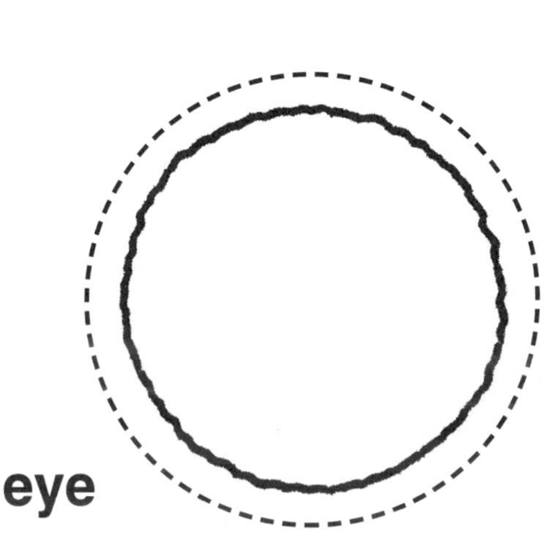

eye

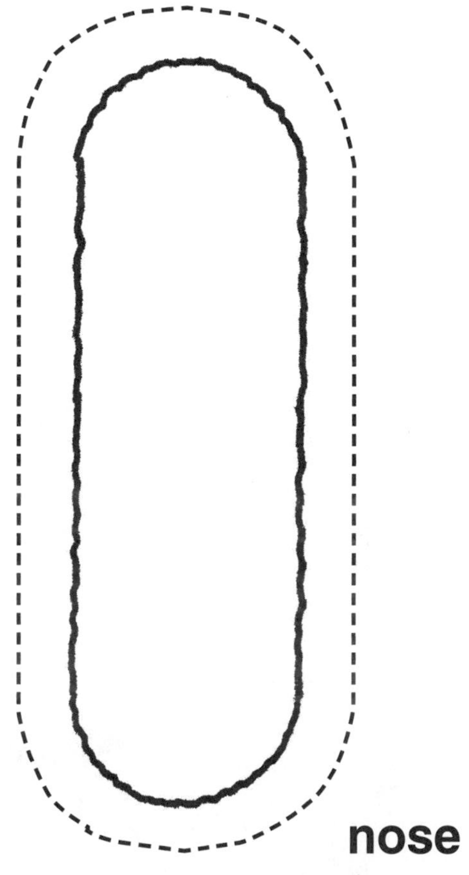

nose

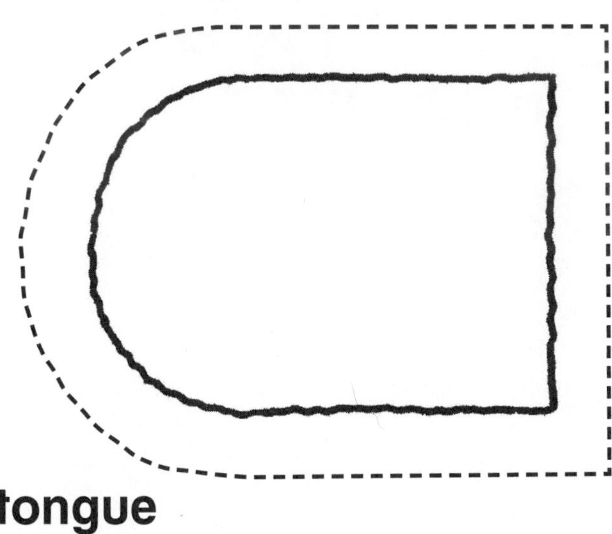

tongue

pupil

Name

Missing Letters

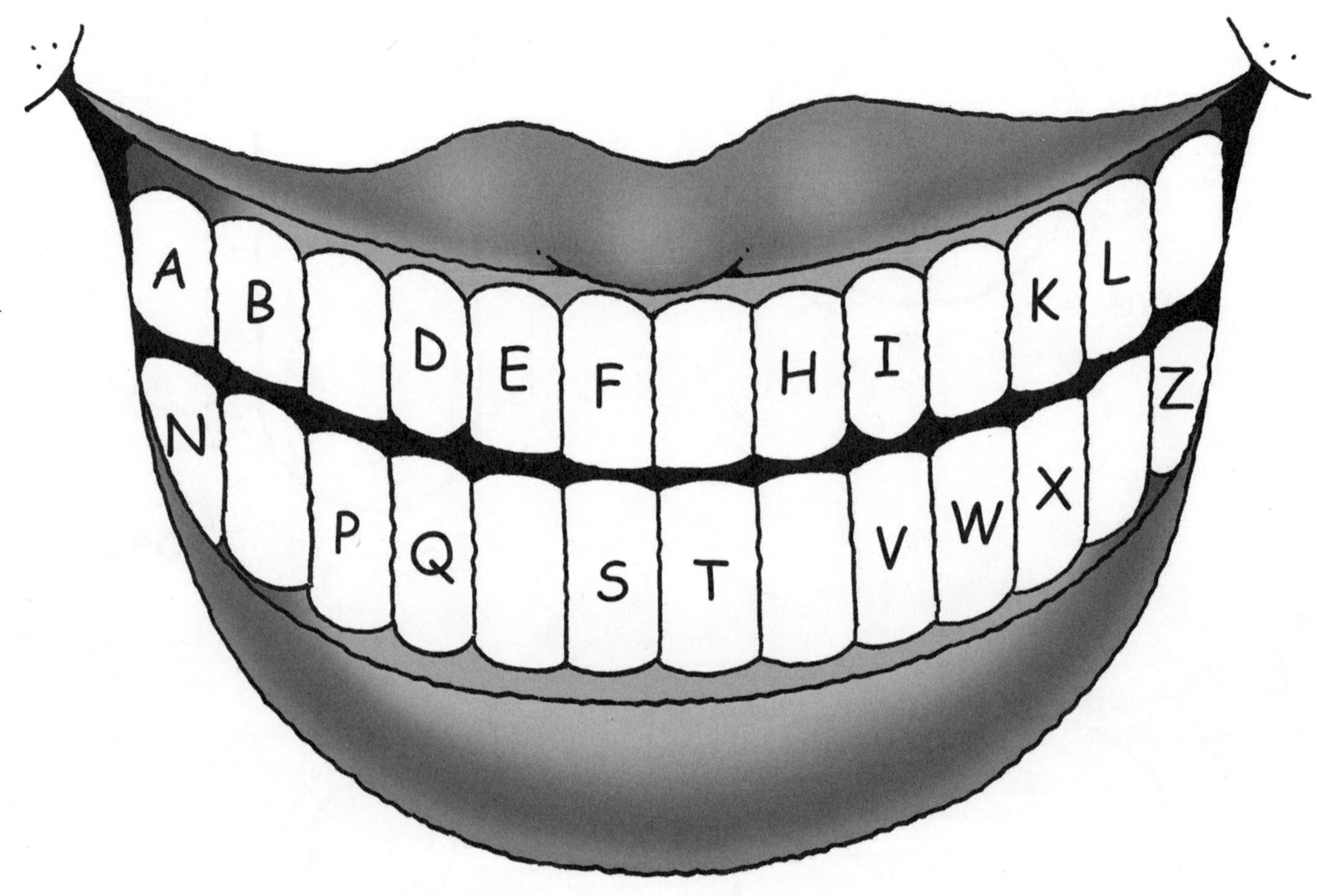

Directions: Use with "The ABC's of Teeth" on page 45. Invite children to write the missing letters.

Name

Tooth Count

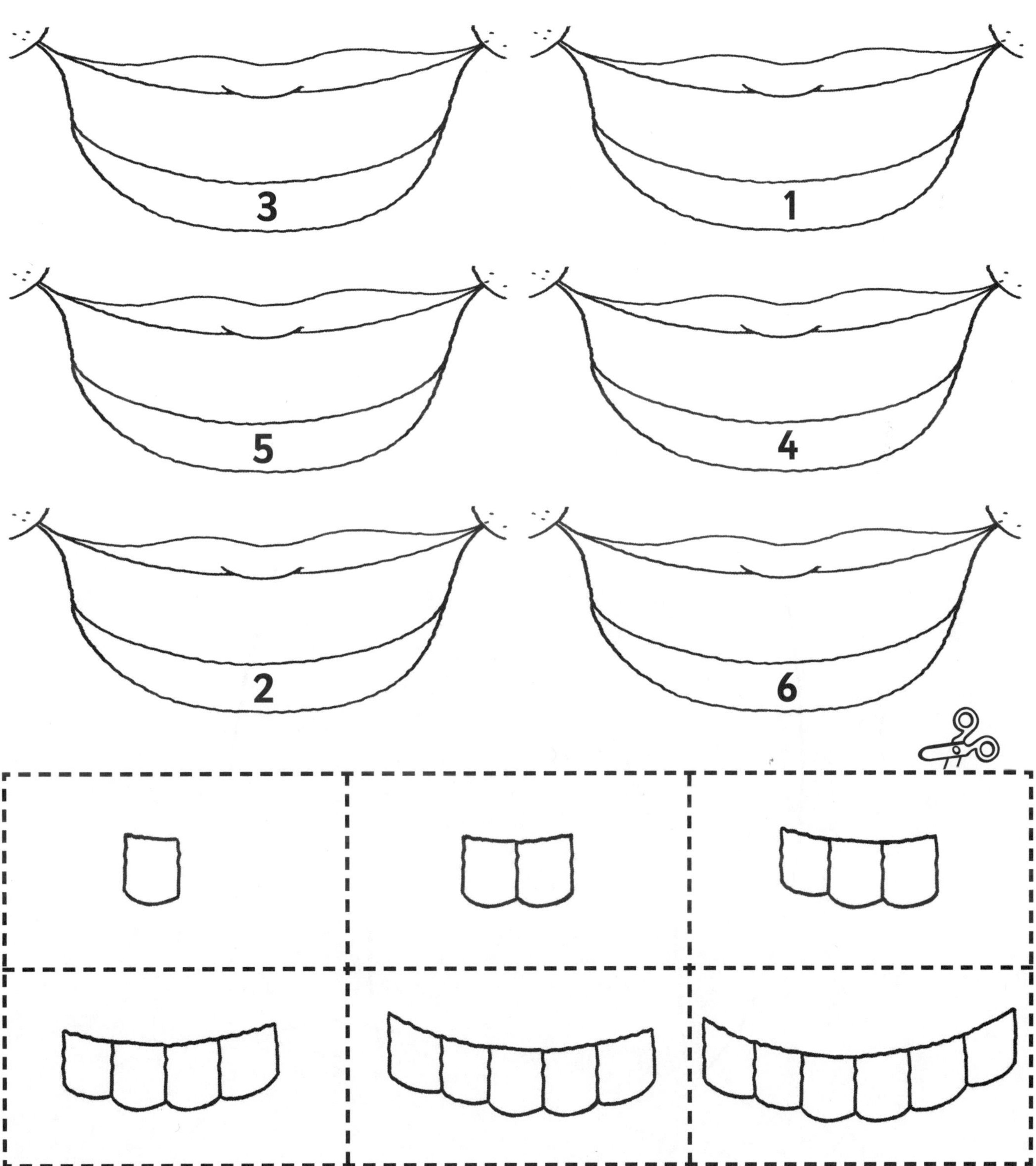

Directions: Use with "Tooth Count" on page 45 and with "Visit the Dentist" on page 48. Have children cut out the teeth and glue them in the smile with the corresponding number. Children may wish to color the page.

Name ______________________

Tooth Talk

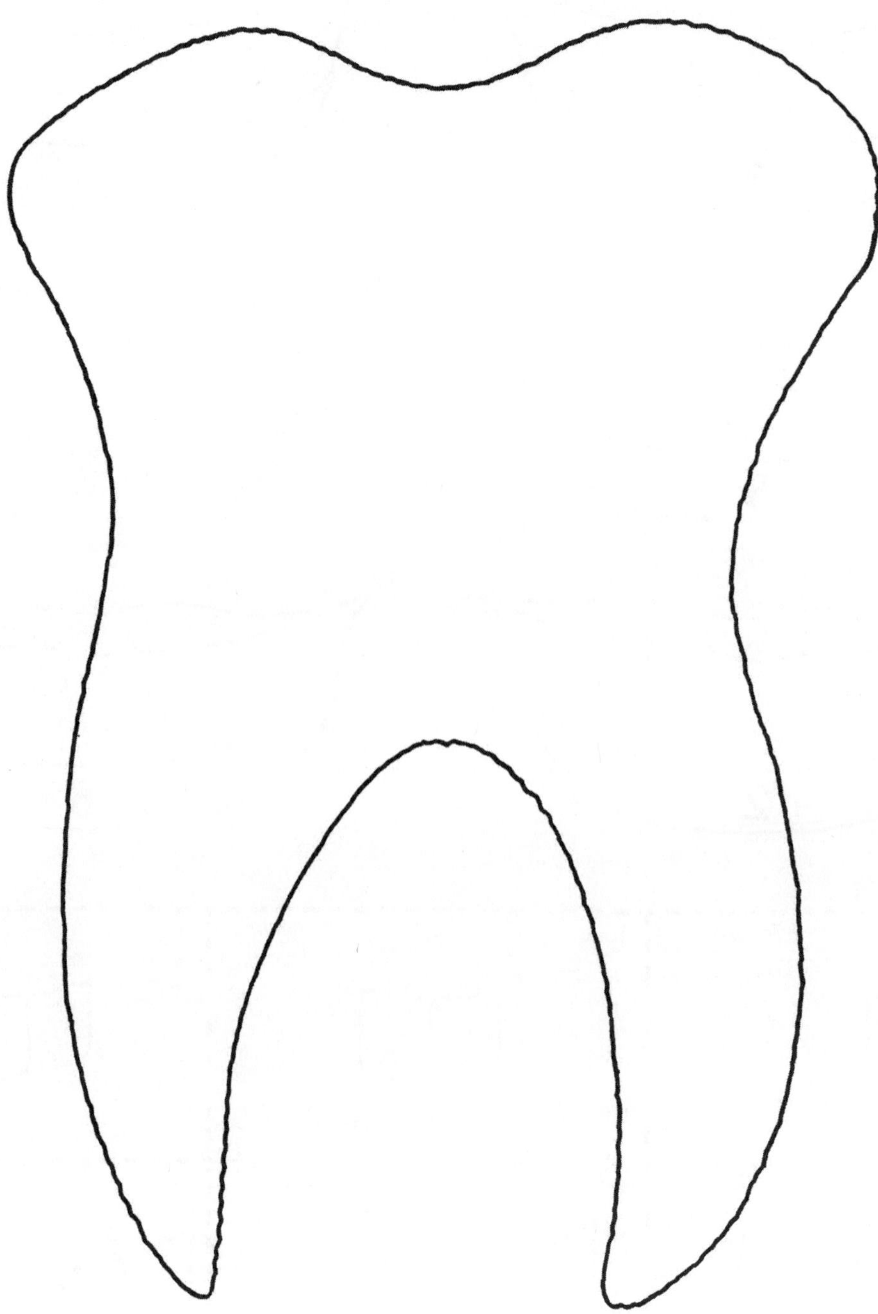

Directions: Use with "Tooth Talk" on page 47. Invite children to draw facial features on the tooth. Then ask them to write or dictate a sentence telling what advice their tooth would tell everyone about taking good care of their teeth.

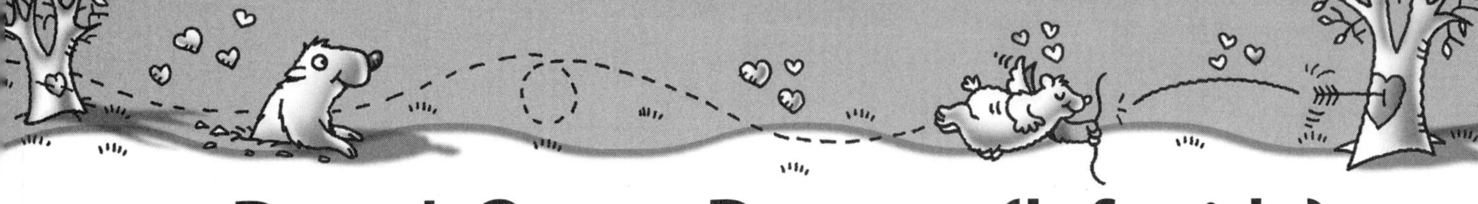

Board Game Pattern (left side)

Use with "Visit the Dentist" on page 48.

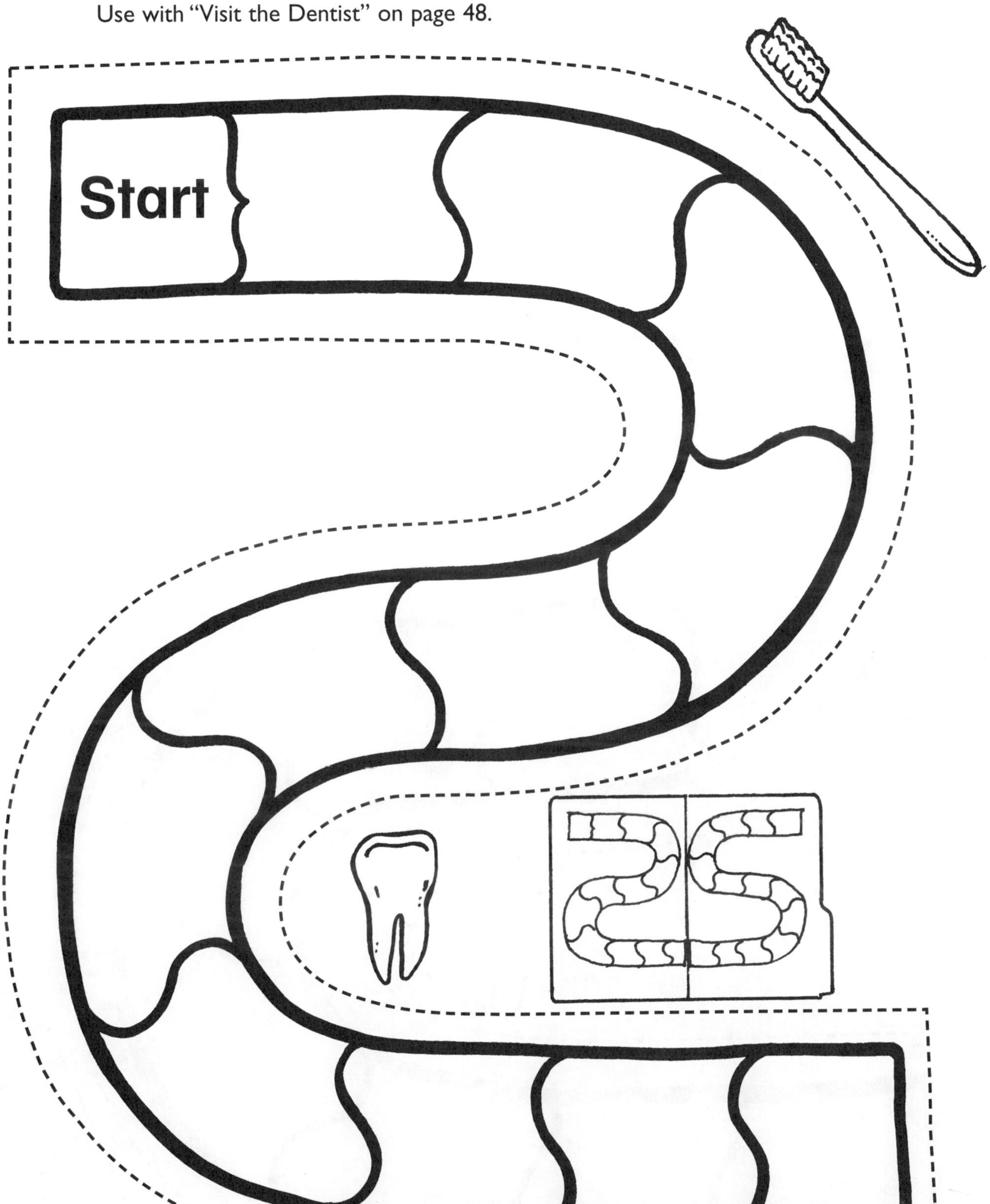

Start

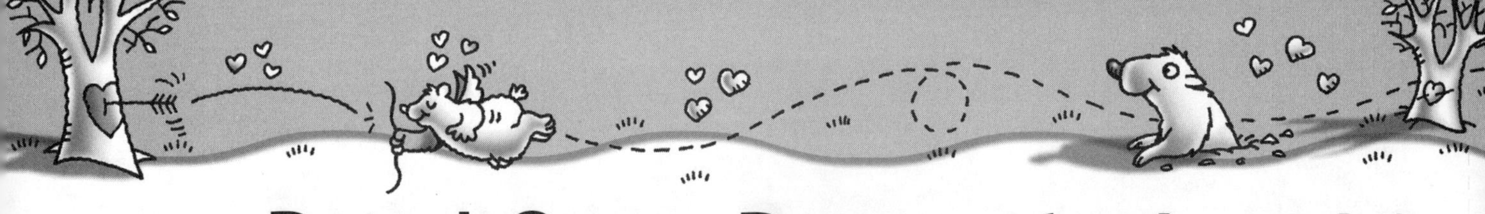

Board Game Pattern (right side)

Use with "Visit the Dentist" on page 48.

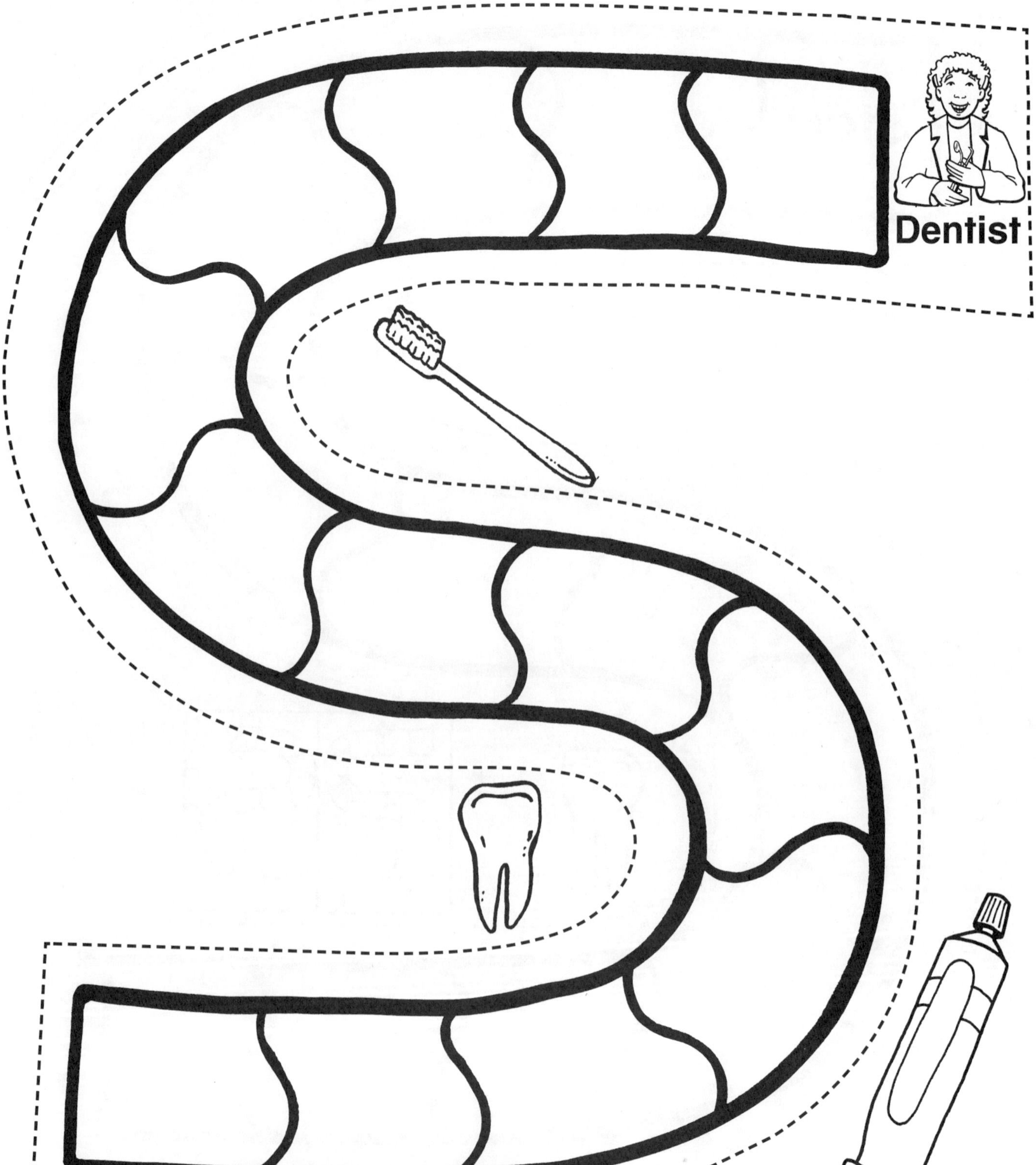

Dentist

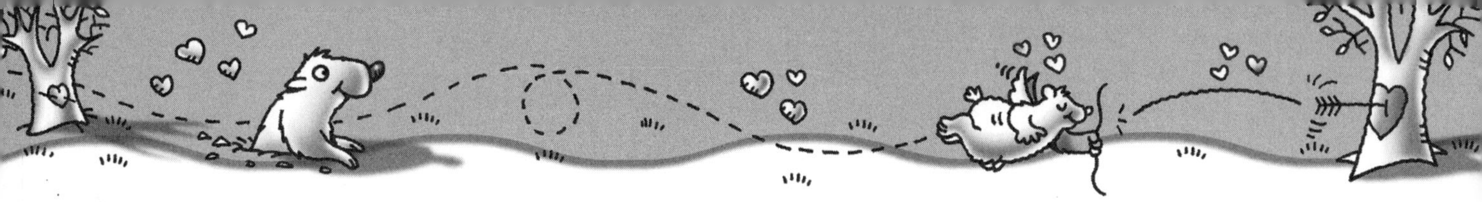

Circus Talk

Circuses began in ancient Rome and included lions, elephants, chariot races, and athletic performances on horses.

Traveling performers went from town to town in Medieval times and showcased acrobatics, horse riding, and trained animals.

The court jester was one of the first kinds of clowns. This person often juggled, sang, and did routines to make the audience laugh.

The circus, as we know it, began with the exciting performances of a British cavalry soldier named Philip Astley around 1768. He traveled around England showing his riding prowess. At one point, he roped off an area into a circle, so that he could stand on a moving horse. This gave rise to the first ring. Astley added clowns to the show in between the horse performances.

The traveling circus began in America in the early 1800's. The group would stop their wagons on the edge of town and pitch tents.

Hackaliah Bailey put together a traveling circus that included an elephant named Old Bet. The animal was a huge success, so Bailey added other exotic animals to the show.

Most circuses have live bands. They lead the circus parade and help set the mood.

The slapstick humor and oversized clothing characteristic of clowns first became popular in Germany. According to one story, a circus performer was confined to his room. He put on some extra large clothing and mimicked the circus owner while some friends were visiting. The owner walked in, and the circus performer ran out of his room, entering the ring accidentally. As he hurried, the man tripped over the ring on the way in and again on the way out. The audience, thinking it was part of the performance, cheered.

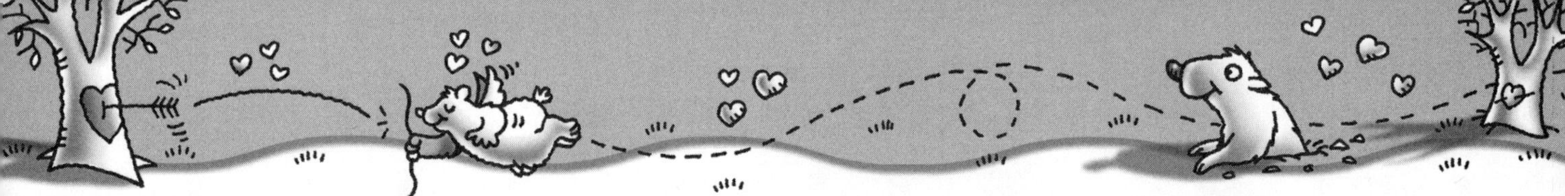

Clown Hat

Materials

- pattern on page 64
- paper plates
- markers or crayons
- scissors
- file folder
- tape
- circle stickers
- glue
- yarn in a variety of bright colors
- construction paper in a variety of bright colors
- wax paper

Directions

Teacher Preparation: Cut out half circles from different colors of construction paper using the cone hat pattern. Cut out the center circle from the plates and discard it. Wind yarn around a file folder multiple times and cut it at the top and bottom to make pieces of hair.

1. Color the top and bottom of a paper plate.
2. With the bottom of the plate facing up, glue yarn around three-fourths of the plate's rim to make hair. Set on a piece of wax paper to dry.
3. Put stickers on the half circle.
4. Bend the half circle so that the straight edges meet to make a cone.
5. Tape the edges together.
6. Glue the tabs from the hat onto the plate to cover the hole.

Clown Bowtie

Materials

- 9" x 11" construction paper in a variety of colors
- large paper clips
- circle stickers
- pipe cleaners

Directions

1. Put stickers on one side of a piece of construction paper.
2. Turn the paper over so that the stickers are facedown.
3. Starting on the long edge, fold the paper about one inch and press to make a straight crease.
4. Turn the paper over and fold the paper another inch.
5. Continue the process to accordion pleat the whole paper to make a bowtie.
6. Twist a pipe cleaner around the middle of the strip so that the knot is on the backside of the bowtie.
7. Push a paper clip over the knot. Children can clip the bowtie to their shirts.

Clown Face Bagel

You will need

- bagels
- spreadable cream cheese
- alfalfa sprouts
- orange sandwich cheese
- sliced green olives
- cherry tomatoes
- yellow bell peppers
- green bell peppers
- paper plates
- craft sticks
- spoons
- knife

Directions

Teacher Preparation: Cut the sliced cheese in half diagonally. Cut the cherry tomatoes in half. Core the yellow and green bell peppers, removing the seeds. Cut the peppers into thin rings. Cut each yellow ring into fourths. Cut each green ring into halves.

1. Spread the cream cheese on half of a bagel.
2. Press the sprouts into the cream cheese on each side of the bagel to make hair.
3. Add a triangle cheese hat.
4. Add two olive eyes.
5. Add a cherry tomato nose.
6. Add a yellow bell pepper mouth.
7. Add a green bell pepper neck ruff.

Note: Be aware of children who may have food allergies.

Circus Want to Be

(Sing to the tune of "The Oscar Meyer Wiener Jingle®.")

I want to be a clown in the circus.
That is what I truly want to be.
And if I was a clown in the circus,
Then everyone would cheer and clap for me!

I want to be a lion in the circus.
That is what I truly want to be.
And if I was a lion in the circus,
Then everyone would cheer and clap for me!

Other circus performers:
I want to be an acrobat in the circus.
I want to be a strongman in the circus.
I want to be a seal in the circus.
I want to be a horse in the circus.

Clown Around with These Books

Carousel
by Donald Crews (Greenwillow)

Circus
by Lois Ehlert (HarperCollins Juvenile Books)

Emeline at the Circus
by Marjorie Priceman (Dragonfly)

If I Ran the Circus
by Dr. Seuss (Random House Books for Young Readers)

Last Night I Dreamed a Circus
by Maya Gottfried (Knopf House Books for Young Readers)

Olivia Saves the Circus
by Ian Falconer (Atheneum)

Paddington Bear at the Circus
by Michael Bond (HarperCollins)

Peter Spier's Circus
by Peter Spier (Dragonfly)

The Circus Is in Town!

Materials

- patterns on page 64
- patterns on page 65
- brightly colored craft paper
- border
- clean meat trays
- black yarn
- black construction paper
- recycled animal magazines
- children's pictures
- hole punch
- markers
- scissors
- glue
- masking tape

Directions

Teacher Preparation: Cover the board with the craft paper. Add a festive border and the caption. Cut out a train engine and a caboose from construction paper using the patterns. Decorate the trains with markers. Cut out the clown outlines. Punch parallel holes along the tops and bottoms of the long sides of the trays for animal cars. Cut out 2-inch circles from the black paper for wheels.

Animal Cars

1. Find and cut out a picture of an animal that would be in a circus.
2. Glue the animal to the inside of the meat tray.
3. Starting on one side, thread the yarn through a hole. Leave about a foot of yarn hanging free in the back.
4. Pull the yarn straight down across the front of the tray and thread the yarn through the opposite hole to make a bar.
5. Thread the yarn through the hole to the left or right.
6. Pull the yarn straight up again to make another bar.
7. Continue making cage bars with the yarn.
8. On the last hole, tie the threads together on the back of the tray.
9. Glue two wheels on the bottom of the animal car.

Clown Cars

1. Choose a clown outline.
2. Glue a child's picture to the clown.
3. Use markers to add details to the clown.
4. Glue the clown to the bottom of the meat tray with two other completed clowns.
5. Glue two wheels on the bottom of the clown car.

Help children tape their cars to the bulletin board. Add the engine and caboose to the train.

Under the Big Top Centers

Math Center

Math Standard
Reads numbers to 10

Hide-and-Seek Numbers

Materials

- activity master on page 66
- crayons

Teacher Preparation: Duplicate the activity master.

Have children find and color the numbers from 0 to 10 using the same color crayon. Then invite them to color the picture.

Language Center

Language Arts Standard
Identifies final sounds

Having a Ball with Letters

Materials

- patterns on page 67
- markers
- file folder
- glue

Teacher Preparation: Duplicate, color, and cut out the seals and the balls patterns. Glue the seals on the inside of a file folder. Write a capital letter on each seal. Write the corresponding lowercase letters on the balls.

Have children find which ball balances on each seal's nose by matching the lowercase letters to the capital letters.

Extension: For a phonemic awareness activity, draw or cut out pairs of pictures whose names have the same ending sounds. For example, cut out magazine pictures of a train and a clown. Glue one picture on a seal and the other on a ball. Children match the ball to a seal by listening for the ending /n/ sound.

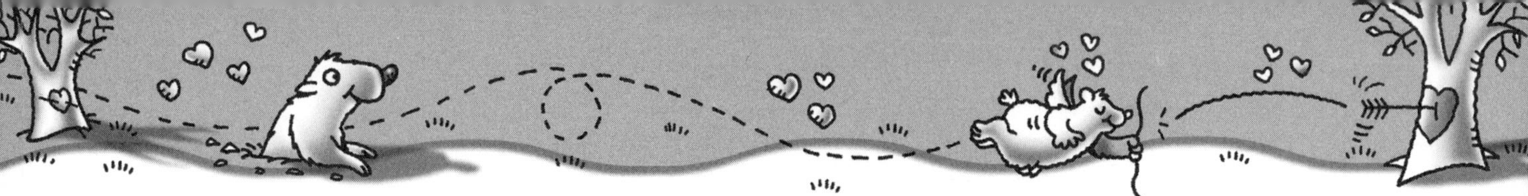

Under the Big Top Centers

Dramatic Play Center

Language Arts Standard
Uses simple sentences to communicate thoughts and ideas when speaking

The Circus Show

Materials

- parachute or colorful umbrella
- 2 large paper bags
- wooden dowel
- masking tape
- scarves
- newspaper
- black spray paint
- balance beam
- circus costumes, such as ballet, clown, ringmaster
- clown hat and bowtie (completed in "Clown Hat" and "Clown Bowtie" on page 56)

Teacher Preparation: Hang the parachute or umbrella above the center to be the circus tent. Make a barbell by filling the paper bags with crumpled newspapers and wrapping the openings around the ends of the dowel. Tape a bag to the end of each dowel and spray paint the dowel and the bags. If a balance beam is not available, make a tape line on the floor to serve as a high wire.

Invite children to role-play circus performers. Clowns can juggle scarves. Acrobats can do amazing tricks on the high wire, and the strong person can lift heavy weights. Ask children who their favorite circus performers are and to explain why.

Block Center

Math Standard
Uses familiar manipulatives to recognize shapes and their relationships

Animals in the Rings

Materials

- circus animal toys
- hoops

Teacher Preparation: Have children use the hoops and blocks to make performing rings and stands. Encourage them to have circus shows with the animals.

Under the Big Top Centers

Writing Center

Language Arts Standard
Uses letters to represent words

Join the Circus

Materials

- activity master on page 68
- crayons
- pencils

Teacher Preparation: Duplicate the activity master.

Review the many kinds of acts children see in a circus. Then ask children what job they would like to have. Have them draw a picture of themselves as their favorite circus performer. Then have them dictate or write a word or words to complete the sentence frame.

Science Center

Science Standard
Understands position and motion of objects

Circus Forces

Materials

- index cards
- crayons
- activity master on page 69
- push toys, such as a lawnmower, a ball, spinning top, and shovel
- pull toys, such as a wagon, duck on a string, and rake

Teacher Preparation: Duplicate the activity master. Write the labels *push* and *pull* on index cards.

Display a push toy and a pull toy. Discuss how a push or a pull is needed to make each toy move. Explain that a force is a push or a pull, and a force is needed to make something move. Then lead children in a discussion of circus activities that show a push or a pull force. In the center, have children sort push and pull toys and put them in labeled groups. Then have children color each picture and circle the word that shows the force.

Under the Big Top Centers

Art Center

Math Standard
Identifies right and left hand

A Handy Clown

Materials

- patterns on page 64
- tempera paints
- wet paper towels
- glue
- construction paper
- clean meat trays
- markers
- 11" x 18" white construction paper
- cotton balls
- sponges
- crayons

Teacher Preparation: Using the clown outline pattern as a guide, trace a large clown face and hat on white construction paper for each child. You may wish to add ears as well. Then place a sponge in each tray and pour different colors of paint over each sponge.

Have children draw the facial features on the clown and decorate the hat. Have them glue a cotton ball to the top of the hat. Then invite them to use their hands to paint the hair and neck ruff. Have children use the left hand to make the hair on the left side of the clown. Have children use the right hand to make the hair on the right side of the clown. Children can use either hand to make the ruff along the bottom of the face.

Game Center

Math Standard
Compares groups and recognizes more than and less than

Animal Training

Materials

- hoops
- red streamers
- stuffed animals
- tape

Teacher Preparation: Cut and tape red streamers to the top of the hoop to make a ring of fire.

Invite children to be animal trainers and help the animals learn to jump through a ring of fire. Children can take turns holding the hoop, or they can lean the hoop against a wall. Have children toss the animals through the hoop. Ask how many children tossed less than two animals through the hoop and how many tossed more than two.

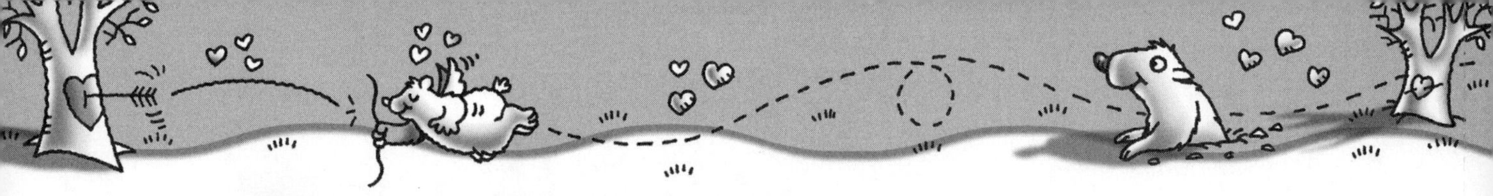

Clown Patterns

Use the cone hat pattern with "Clown Hat" on page 56. Use the clown outline patterns with "The Circus Is in Town!" on page 59 and with "A Handy Clown" on page 63.

tab

tab

tab

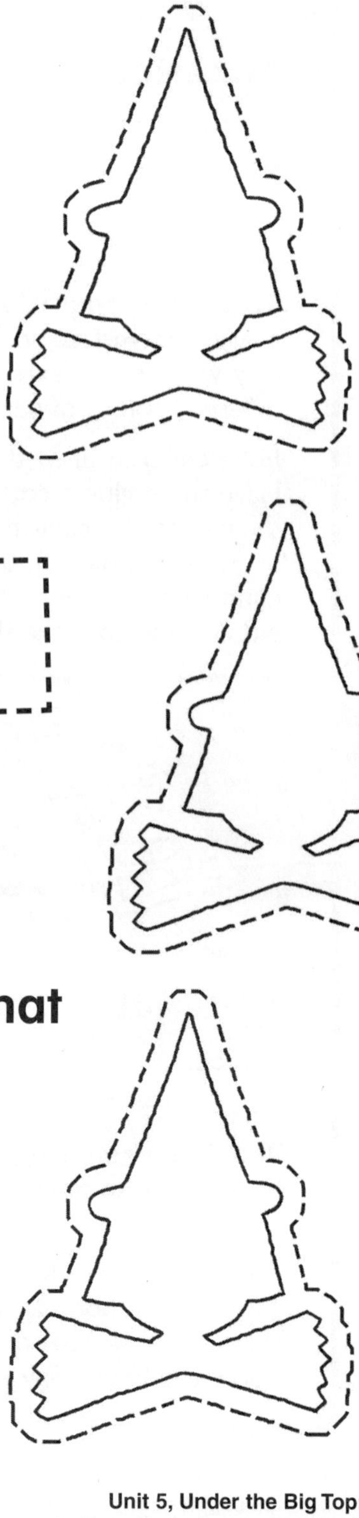

cone hat

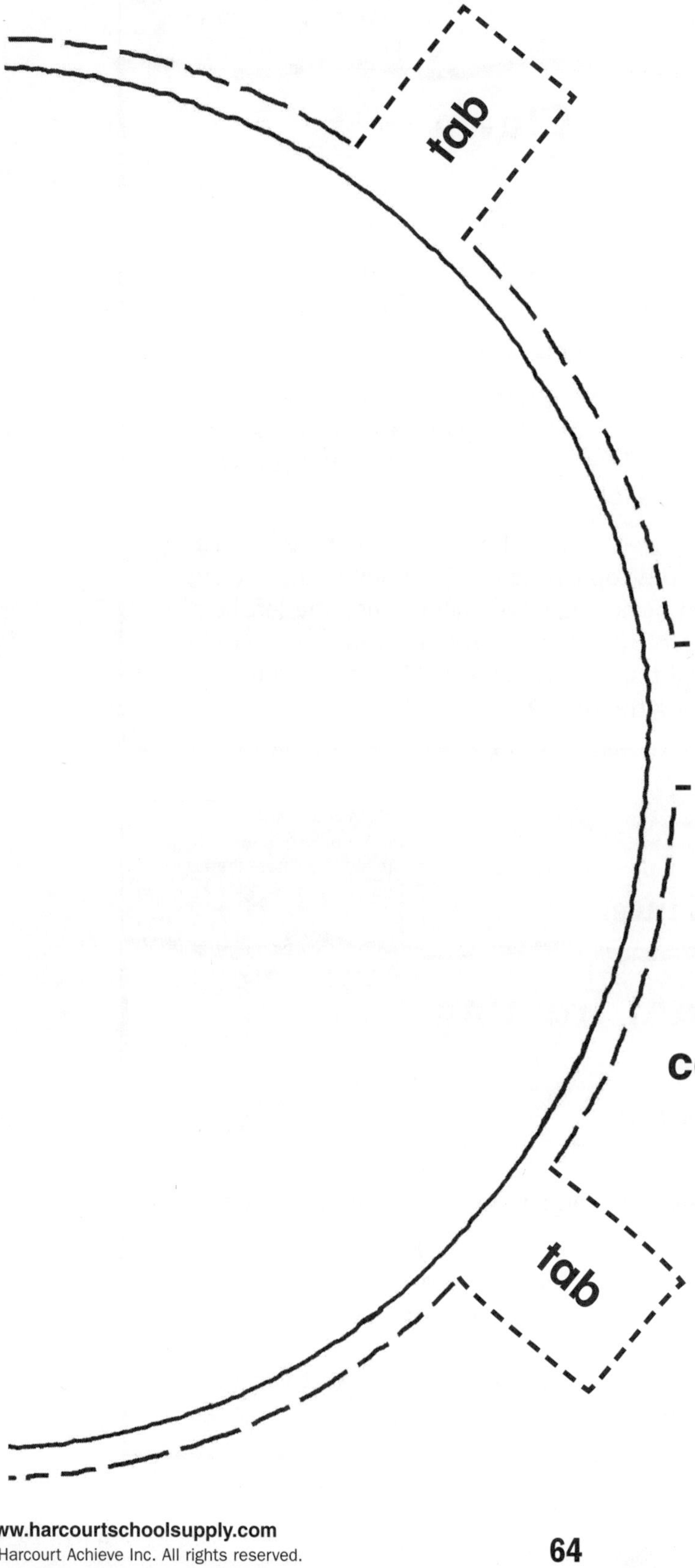

clown outlines

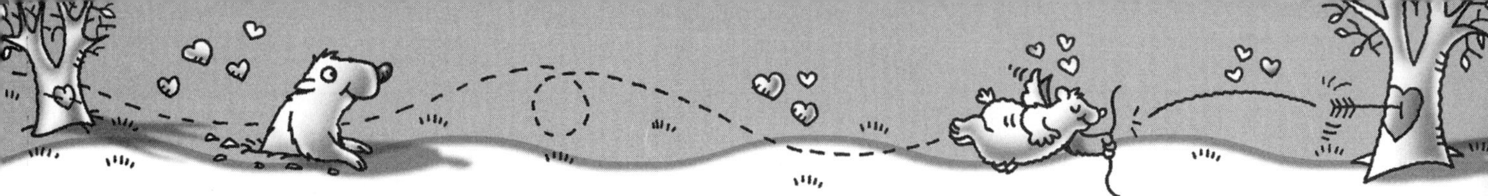

Train Patterns

Use with "The Circus Is in Town!" on page 59.

engine

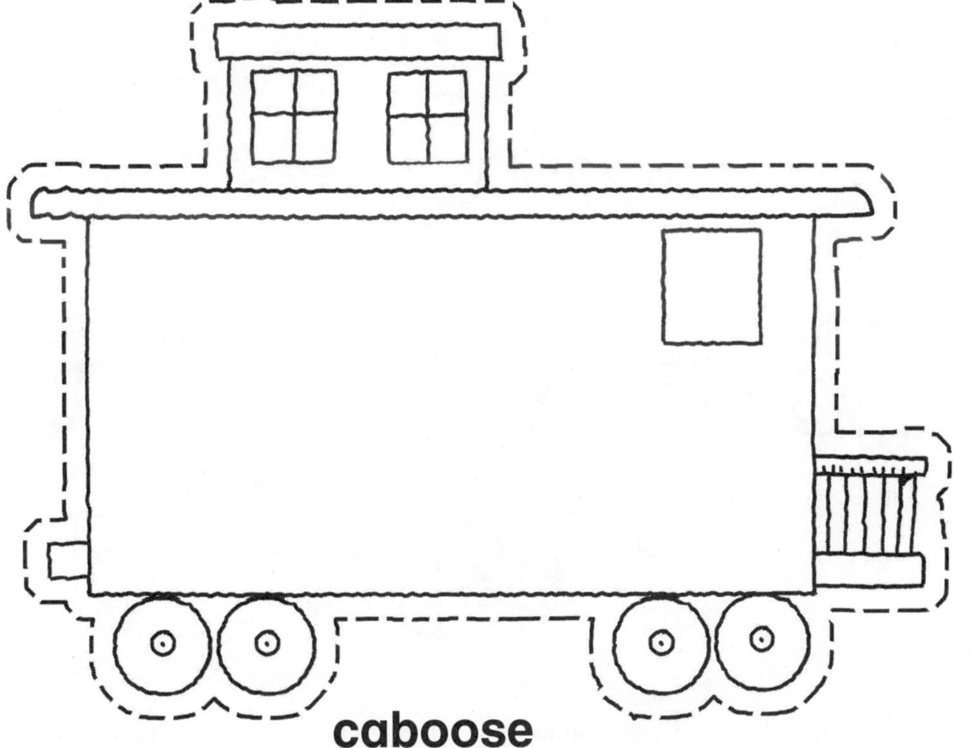

caboose

Name

Circus Number Fun

Directions: Use with "Hide-and-Seek Numbers" on page 60. Have children find and color the numbers from 0 to 10 using the same color crayon. Then invite them to color the picture.

Name

Push or Pull

push pull

push pull

Directions: Use with "Circus Forces" on page 62. Have children color each picture and circle the word that shows the force.

Shop Talk

2¢ Long ago people bartered, or traded, to get the goods they needed. They bartered animals, produce, leather, and even sugar.

2¢ When gold and silver were used to buy things, the metal was made into lumps, nuggets, and bars. The bars were large and heavy to carry. Also, there was no way to tell if the gold or silver was pure or if it was mixed with another, cheaper metal.

2¢ The Greeks were the first to make coins. The coins showed pictures of the deity animals they worshipped.

2¢ A numismatist is a person who studies and collects coins and paper money.

2¢ A craftsman was a man or woman who made things, such as shoes, jewelry, or silver dishes. They worked in small shops. The craftsman would choose a boy or girl to live with the family for many years and teach the craft to the child. The child was an apprentice. During the winter months, the people made the goods. In the spring and summer, the older apprentices would load up a wagon with the goods and go from town to town and house to house to sell or trade the goods.

2¢ Eventually, the craftsmen got other people, called *peddlers*, to travel to different places to sell their goods. This way, the apprentice could stay home and work.

2¢ Many towns long ago held market days. On an assigned day of the week or month, people would bring their goods to a central place in the town. They would set up a stall, or small booth, and display their goods. These events were festive times and would attract traveling performers.

2¢ Many cultures around the world still sell goods they make and grow in outdoor markets.

2¢ One of the earliest shopping malls was built in Paris in 1784. It was a large area with a five-story palace on one side. It had stores, eating places, fountains, apartments, and gardens.

2¢ The first enclosed shopping center opened in Italy in 1878. It was a glass covered, four-story building.

Box Stores

Materials

- shoe boxes
- craft paper
- magazines
- markers
- glue
- scissors
- tape

Directions

Teacher Preparation: Cover the top and bottom of a shoe box with craft paper. Provide a top and bottom for each child. Cut different colors of craft paper into small rectangle cards for store signs.

1. Choose a kind of store.
2. Draw windows and a door on the outside of the box lid.
3. Draw or cut out pictures of things the store would sell to "display" in the window.
4. Write the name of the store on a card to make a sign.
5. Glue the sign on the outside of the box lid.
6. Cut out pictures of things to sell in the store.
7. Glue the pictures inside the box.

Town Map Mural

Materials

- white craft paper
- tempera paints
- sponge brushes
- containers
- pencil

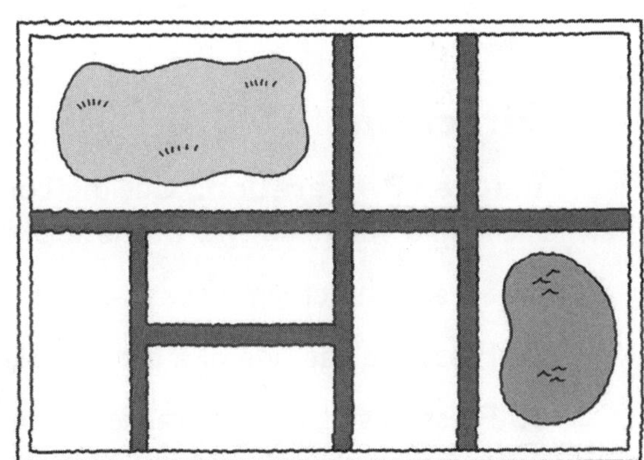

Directions

Teacher Preparation: Sketch a simple town map that shows a series of roads, a park, and a lake. Draw a grid on the map, making the same number of squares as there are children in the class. Write a child's name in each square so that each child will know which area of the mural she or he will paint.

1. Find the square with your name.
2. Paint the different parts of the square.

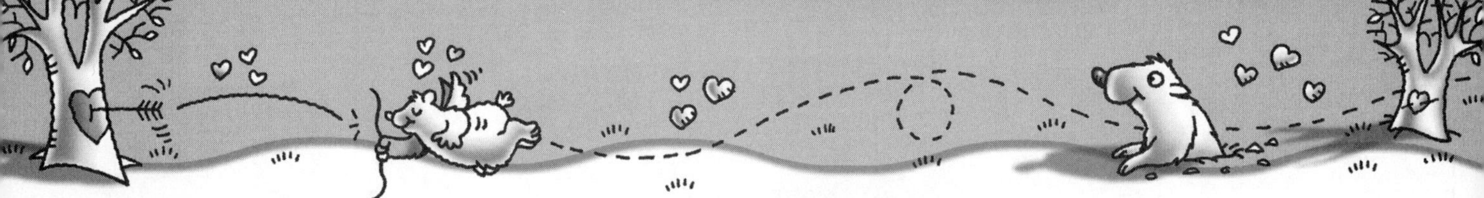

Piggybank Snack

You will need

- rice cakes
- round crackers
- spreadable strawberry cream cheese
- pink and yellow gumdrops
- raisins
- large paper plates
- craft sticks
- knife

Directions

Teacher Preparation: Cut the corners off some pink gumdrops to make triangle shapes. Each child will need two of these. Slice the yellow gumdrops into circles to make coins.

1. Spread the cream cheese on a rice cake and a cracker. Place the rice cake on a paper plate.
2. Press the flat side of a gumdrop in the middle of the cracker to make a nose.
3. Press raisins on the cracker to make the eyes and mouth.
4. Place the cracker on one side of the rice cake to make the head.
5. Dip the uncut edges of two triangle-shaped gumdrops in the cream cheese and press them a little way under the top of the cracker to make the ears as well as support the cracker head.
6. Dip the flat side of two gumdrops into the cream cheese and press them against the side of the rice cake to make legs.
7. Use several raisins to make a line along the top of the rice cake, representing an opening to drop the money.
8. Press two yellow gumdrops beside the line of raisins to make coins.

Note: Be aware of children who may have food allergies.

Mother Went to the Food Store

(Sing to the tune of "The Bear Went over the Mountain.")

Mother went to the food store.
Mother went to the food store.
Mother went to the food store,
To buy some food for us.

Father went to the shoe store.
Father went to the shoe store.
Father went to the shoe store,
To buy some shoes for us.

(Child's name) went to the (product) store.
(Child's name) went to the (product) store.
(Child's name) went to the (product) store,
To buy some (product) for us.

Books Worth Shopping For

Grandpa's Corner Store
by DyAnne Disalvo-Ryan (HarperCollins)

Just Grandpa and Me
by Mercer Mayer (Golden Books)

Mama and Papa Have a Store
by Amelia Lau Carling (Dial Books for Young Readers)

Maisy Goes Shopping
by Lucy Cousins (Candlewick Press)

Not So Fast, Songololo
by Niki Daly (Margaret K. McElderry)

One Present from Flekman's
by Alan Arkin (HarperCollins Juvenile Books)

Who Wants Arthur?
by Amanda Graham (Gareth Stevens Children's Books)

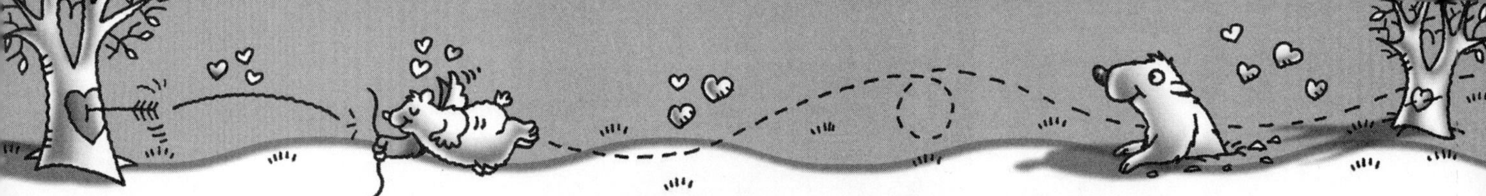

Everything Is Blooming at the Flower Store

Materials

- pattern on page 79
- pattern on page 80
- children's pictures
- craft paper
- overhead projector
- transparency
- tempera paints
- paper baking liners
- green construction paper
- border
- paintbrushes
- scissors
- glue
- stapler
- construction paper (that matches the colors of the liners)

Directions

Teacher Preparation: Make a transparency of the flower store pattern. Cover the board with the craft paper. Use the transparency to trace a large flower store on one side of the bulletin board. Paint the store. Trace and cut out the vases so that they are the same colors as the paper baking liners. Write the color words on the vases and staple the vases to the bulletin board. Add a festive border and the caption.

1. Choose a paper liner for a flower color.
2. Glue a child's picture in the liner.
3. Cut a strip from green paper for the stem.
4. Cut an oval from green paper for a leaf.
5. Glue the flower and leaf on the stem.

Have children match the color of their flowers to the colors of the vases. Help children staple the flowers in the vases.

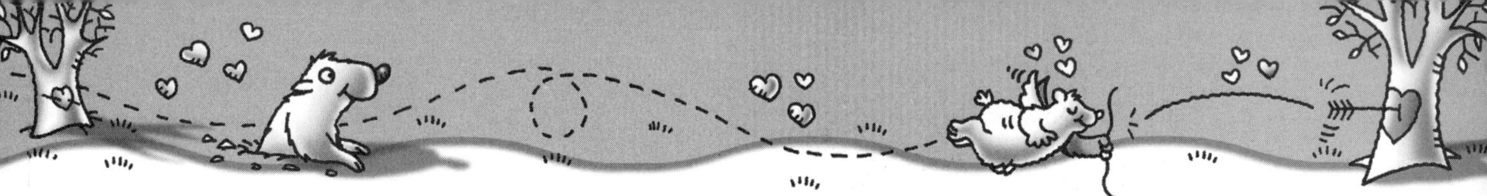

Shopping Centers

Block Center

Math Standard
Uses familiar manipulatives to recognize shapes and their relationships

Going to the Store

Materials

- toy cars
- box stores (completed in "Box Stores" on page 71)
- town mural (completed in "Town Map Mural" on page 71)

Teacher Preparation: Lay the town map on the floor.

Have children place their store boxes on the map. Invite children to build bridges, walls, and other town features with blocks. Then have children drive the cars to the different stores to go shopping.

Art Center

Language Arts Standard
Writes labels and captions

Vegetable Prints

Materials

- paper
- tempera paints
- clean meat trays
- sponges
- vegetables, such as green bell peppers, carrots, ears of corn, broccoli

Teacher Preparation: Cut the vegetables so that the most interesting print can be made. Put a sponge in each tray and pour paint over it. Put one of each vegetable in another tray beside each paint color.

Have children press the vegetables on a sponge and then on the paper. Challenge children to write a label or caption for their creations.

Shopping Centers

Reading Center

Language Arts Standard
Begins to use word recognition strategies, with support

Ads Add Up

Materials

- color advertisements
- crayons
- tape
- scissors
- paper

Teacher Preparation: Tape the advertisements on the wall. Cut the paper into sixths and staple several sheets together to make a notebook for each child.

Ask children to read the advertisements or read the advertisements to them. Have children write words or draw pictures to make a list of things they would like to buy.

Dramatic Play Center

Math Standard
Sorts or classifies by size

Shoe Store

Materials

- old shoes
- shoe polishing equipment
- cash register
- disinfectant spray
- shoe boxes
- mirror
- play money

Teacher Preparation: Set up the center to be a shoe store. Spray disinfectant in the shoes.

Invite children to arrange the shoes by size in order to display them. Then have children role-play selling and buying shoes. The clerk can give the shoes a shine, box up the shoes, and take the customer's money.

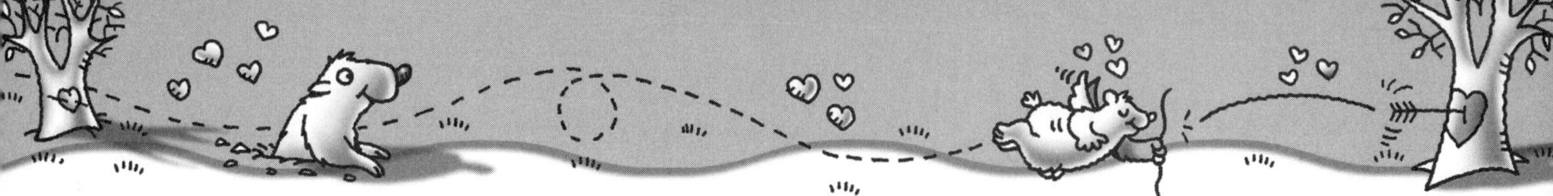

Flower Store Pattern

Use with "Everything Is Blooming at the Flower Store" on page 74.

Flower Store

Sale!

Vase Pattern

Use with "Everything Is Blooming at the Flower Store" on page 74.

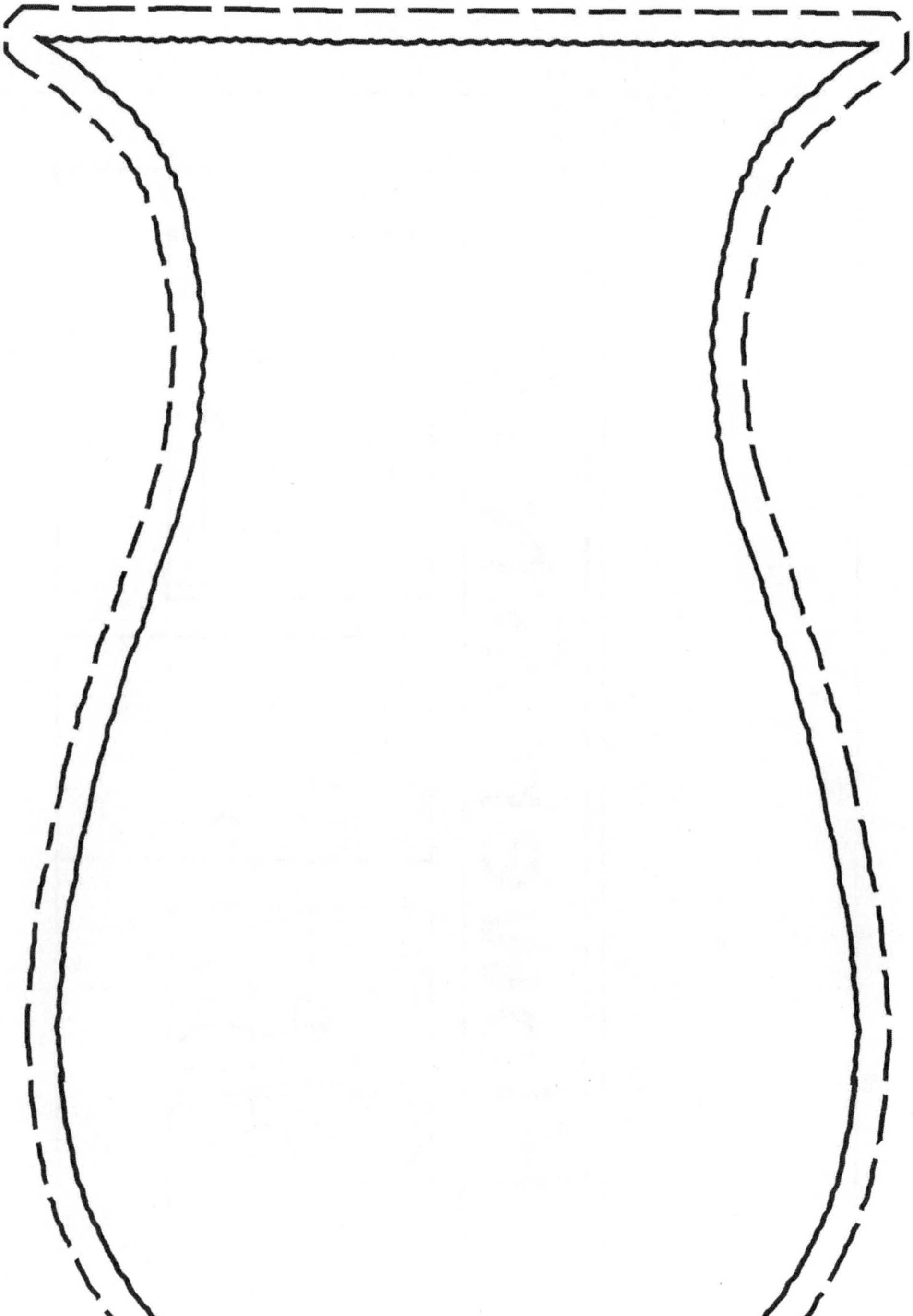

vase

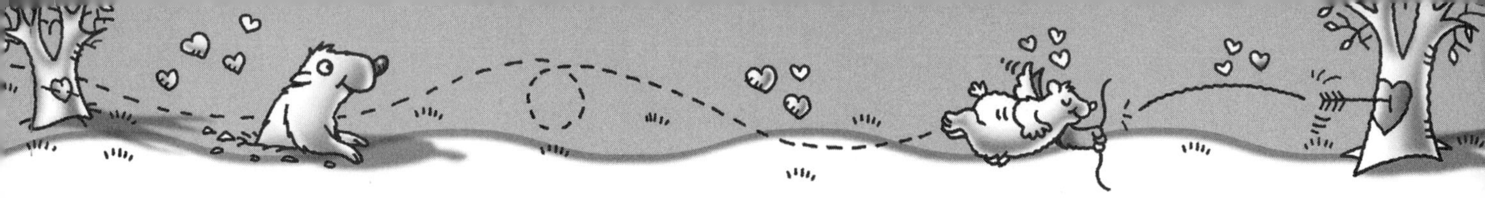

Toy Cards

Use with "Toy Store Matchup" on page 75.

doll	football	kite
bat	fan	jack-in-the-box
bike	duck	jacks

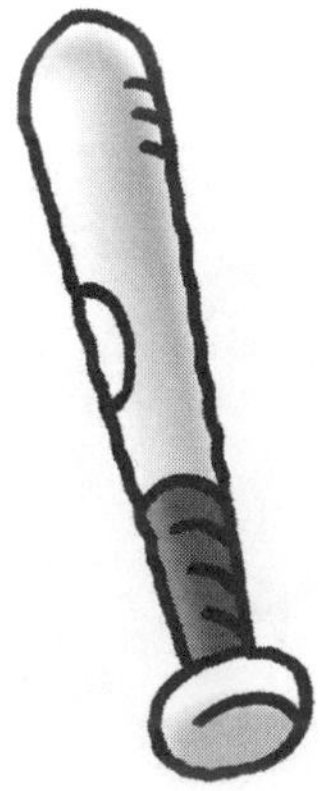

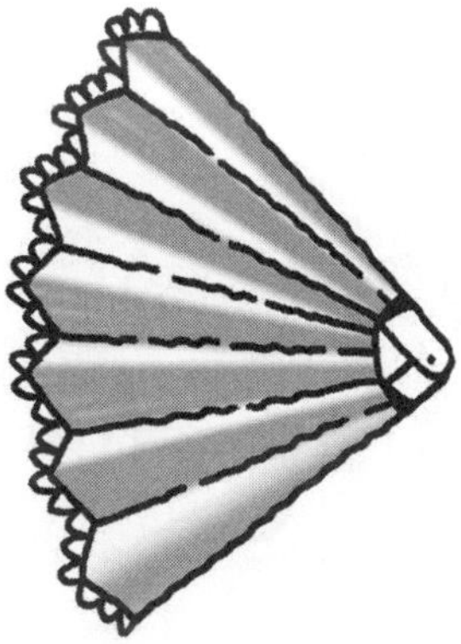

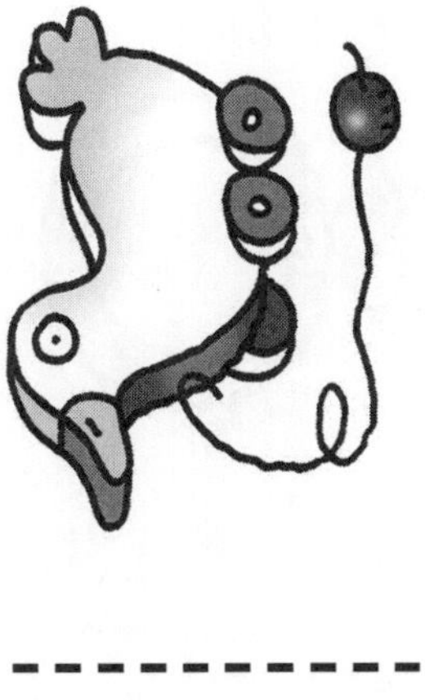

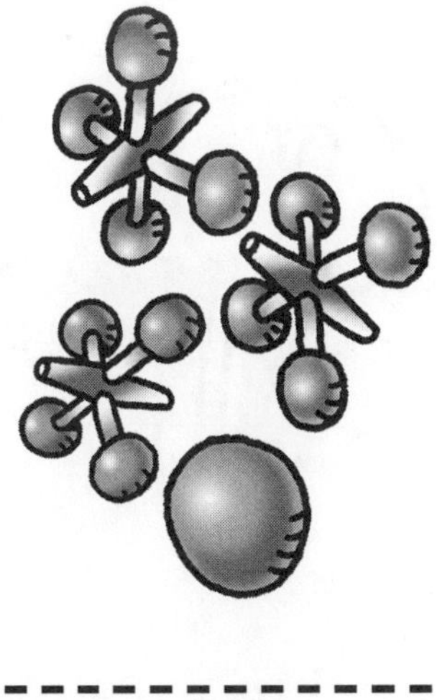

Toy Cards

Use with "Toy Store Matchup" on page 75.

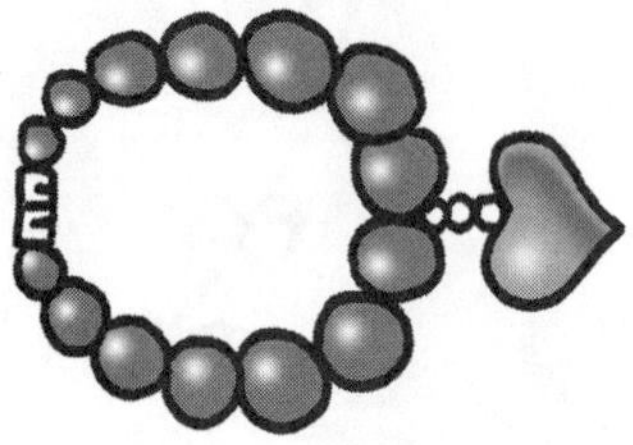

necklace	top	watch
net	robot	wagon
key	ring	tent

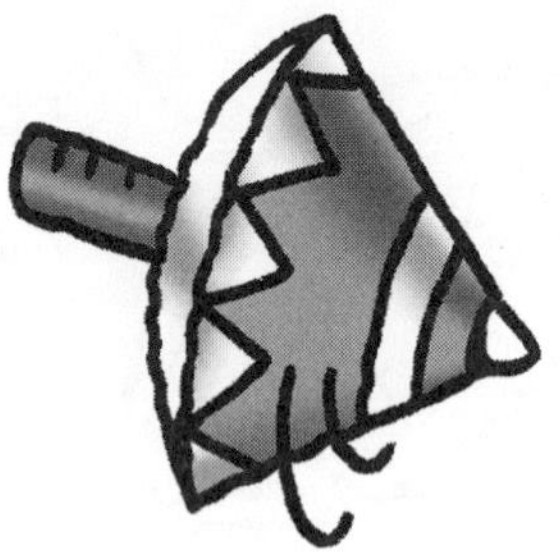

Name ______________________

How Much Does It Cost?

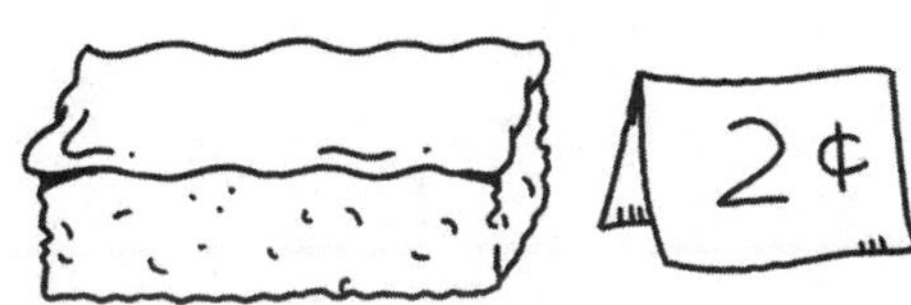

Directions: Use with "Bakery Buys" on page 75. Have children draw lines to match the treat with its cost. Then have them color the page.

Coin Workmat

Use with "Coin Sort" on page 76.

 penny	 nickel
 dime	 quarter

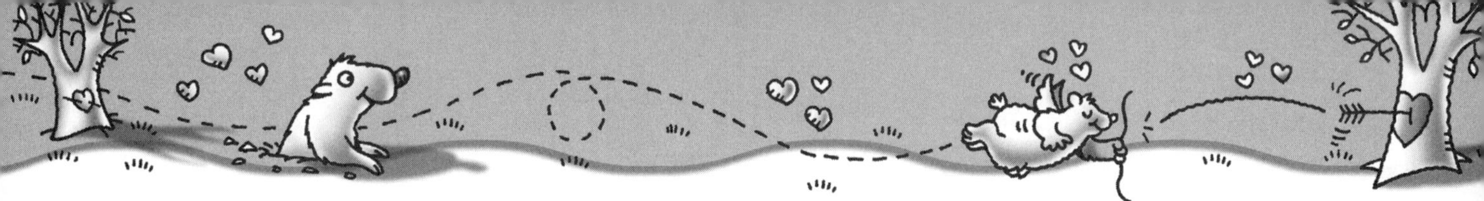

A Look at Anne Rockwell

Anne Rockwell, a well-known children's author and illustrator, was born February 8, 1934, in Memphis, Tennessee.

From childhood, Anne knew that she wanted to draw. So she studied art and sculpting in college.

Before becoming a writer, she held such jobs as a secretary at an advertising firm and an assistant recreation leader in a hospital.

Anne married Harlow Rockwell, a magazine illustrator, and they teamed up to write 26 books together.

In all, Anne has written and/or illustrated more than 100 books.

Anne writes both fiction and nonfiction books for young children, but she tries to focus on nonfiction books for preschool children.

Anne now teams up with her daughter Lizzy. Anne writes the text, and Lizzy draws the pictures.

Over the past five years, Anne has won many commendations for her books.

The book *Valentine's Day* holds special memories for Anne. Anne always made her own valentine cards to give away at school. She also couldn't wait to see who would put a card in her decorated valentine box.

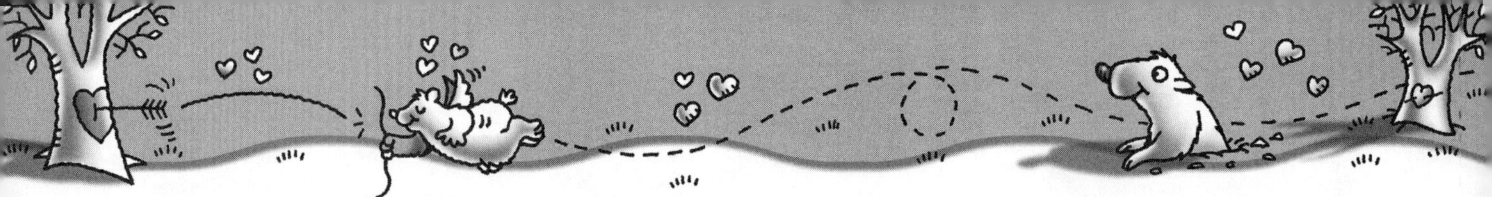

Valentine's Day by Anne Rockwell

Read *Valentine's Day* and point out the author's challenge to find 200 hearts in the book. As you read the book, help children find the hearts on each page. Then have children do the following activities.

Valentine Man

Materials

- patterns on pages 89 and 90
- black, white, yellow, and pink construction paper
- tag board
- crayons
- 12" x 18" red construction paper
- scissors
- glue

Directions

Teacher Preparation: Trace and cut out several heart and hat patterns from tag board.

1. Look on the back cover of the book at the picture of the valentine man.
2. Fold a sheet of red construction paper in half.
3. Place the straight edge of a heart pattern on the fold line. Trace and cut out the heart.
4. Trace and cut out a black hat.
5. Cut four strips of pink paper to make the arms and legs.
6. Accordion pleat the paper strips.
7. Cut a strip of yellow paper for the hatband.
8. Cut out the face parts from construction paper. Be creative!
9. Glue the face parts, arms, legs, hat, and hatband on the valentine man.
10. Write a message on the card.

My Special Valentine

Materials

- activity master on page 91
- construction paper
- art supplies
- crayons or markers
- glue
- scissors

Directions

Teacher Preparation: Duplicate the activity master on construction paper.

Remind children that the students in Mrs. Madoff's class made valentines that reflected a special time that they shared with Michiko. Invite children to think about a special friend and time the two shared. Have them draw and decorate a valentine card for that person. Then have children write or dictate a sentence telling whom the card is for and what they did together.

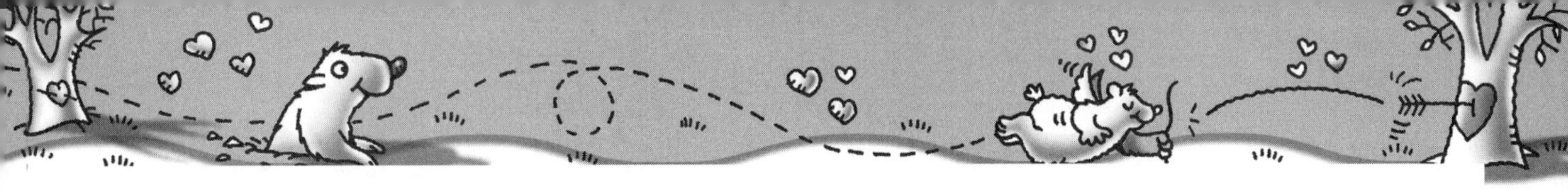

Books by Anne Rockwell

- *100 School Days* (HarperCollins)
- *Career Day* (HarperCollins)
- *Chip and the Karate Kick* (HarperCollins)
- *Come to Town* (HarperTrophy)

This book can be read during the "Let's Go Shopping!" unit.

- *Katie Catz Makes a Splash* (HarperCollins)
- *Mr. Panda's Painting* (Simon & Schuster)

This book can be read during the "Let's Go Shopping!" unit.

- *My Pet Hamster* (HarperTrophy)
- *My Spring Robin* (Aladdin Library)

This book can be read to celebrate Black History Month.

- *Only Passing Through* (Dragonfly)
- *Our Earth* (Voyager Books)
- *Show and Tell Day* (HarperCollins Juvenile Books)

This book can be read during the "Let's Go Shopping!" unit.

- *The Supermarket* (Atheneum)
- *Things That Go* (Puffin)
- *What We Like* (Gale Group)

Bookmark Patterns

What We
Like
are
books
by
Anne
Rockwell!

Heart Pattern

Use with "Valentine Man" on page 86.

fold line

Hat Pattern

Use with "Valentine Man" on page 86.

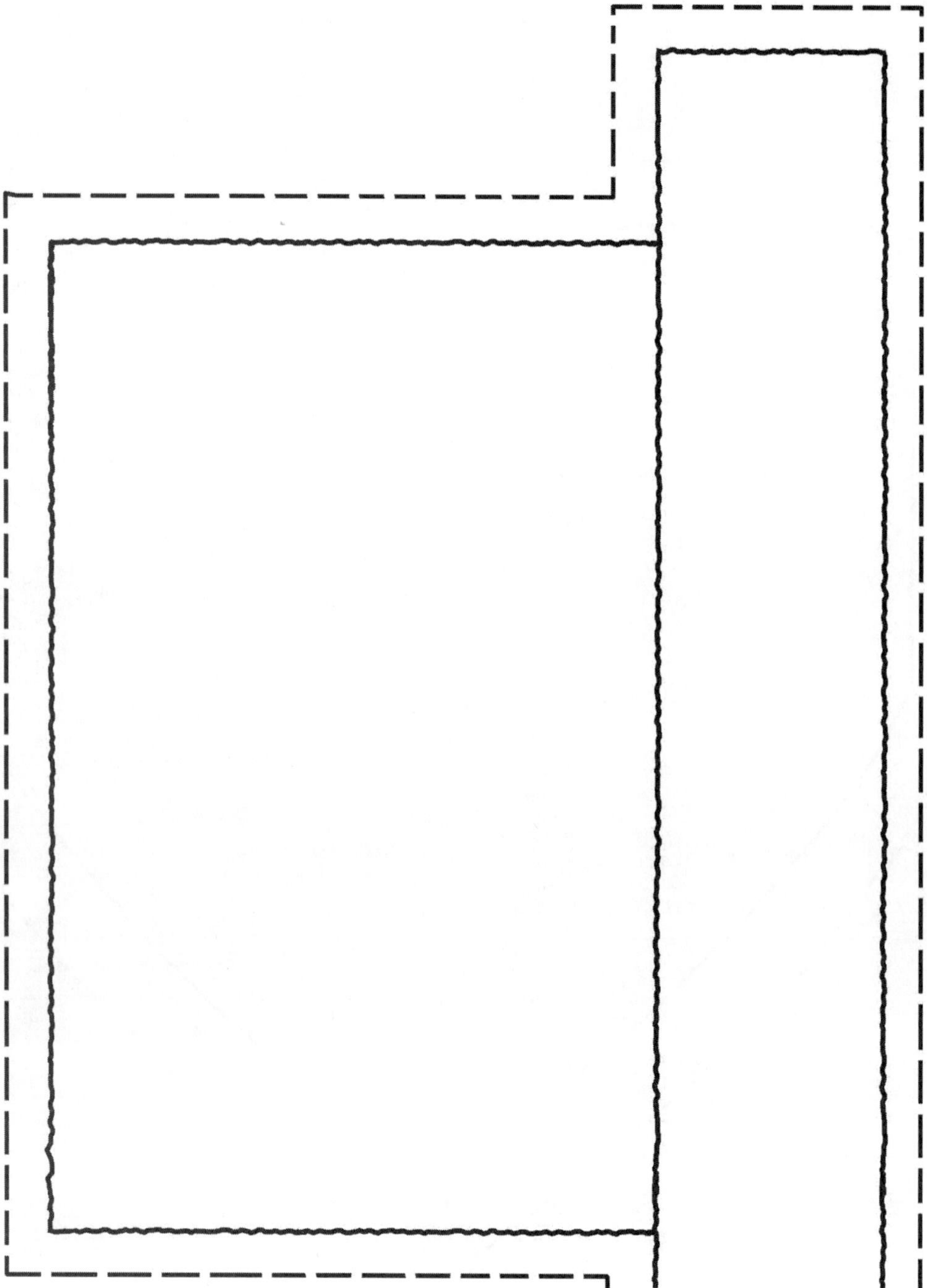

hat

Name

My Special Valentine

My special valentine is for

Together, we

Directions: Use with "My Special Valentine" on page 86. Invite children to think about a special friend and a time the two shared. Have them draw a valentine card for that person. Then have children write or dictate a sentence telling whom the card is for and what they did together.

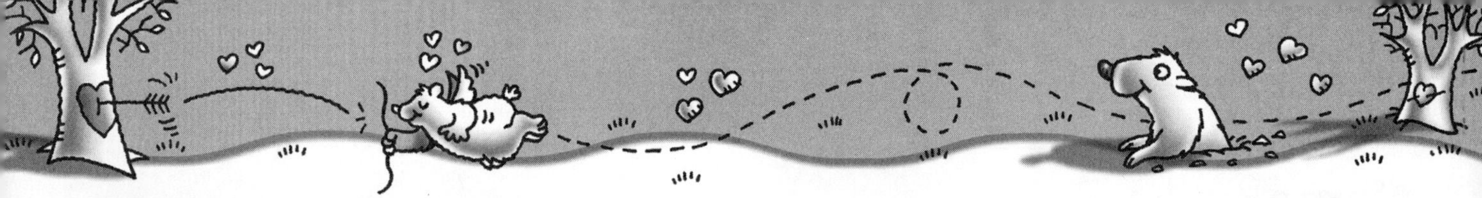

Center Icons

Art Center

Block Center

Dramatic Play Center

Game Center

Center Icons

Language Center

Math Center

Music Center

Puzzle Center

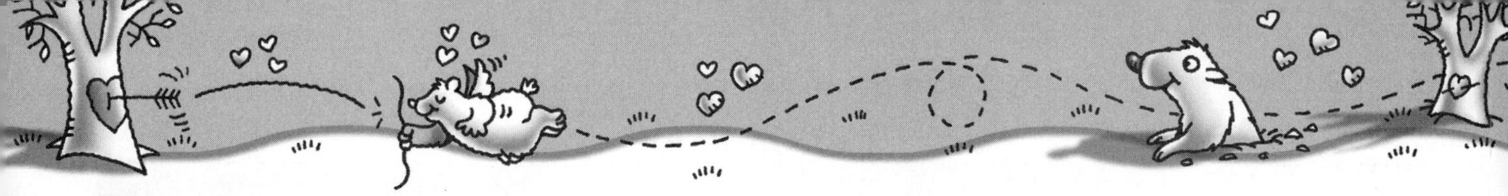

Center Icons

Reading Center

Science Center

Sensory Center

Writing Center

Student Awards

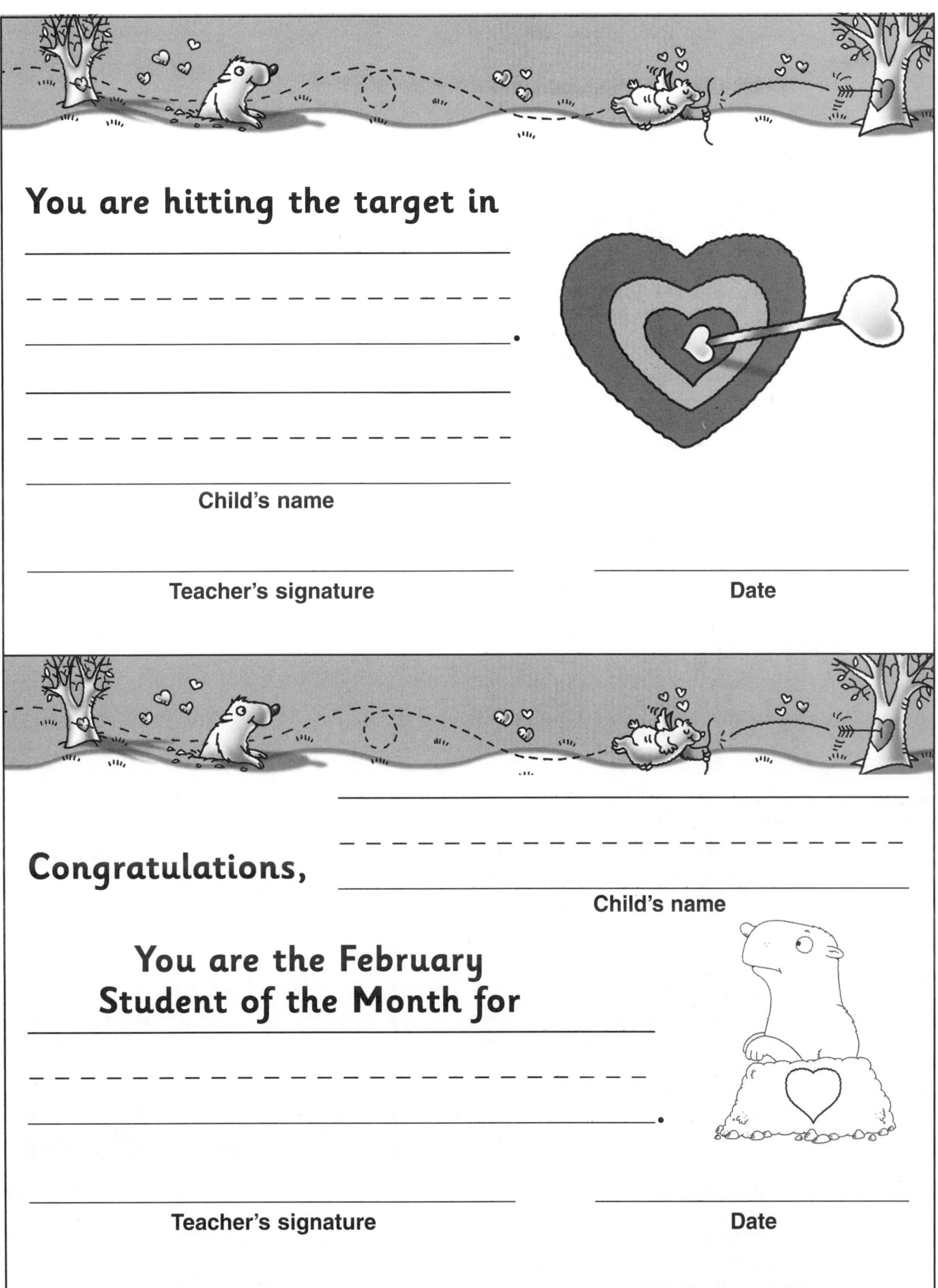

Student Award

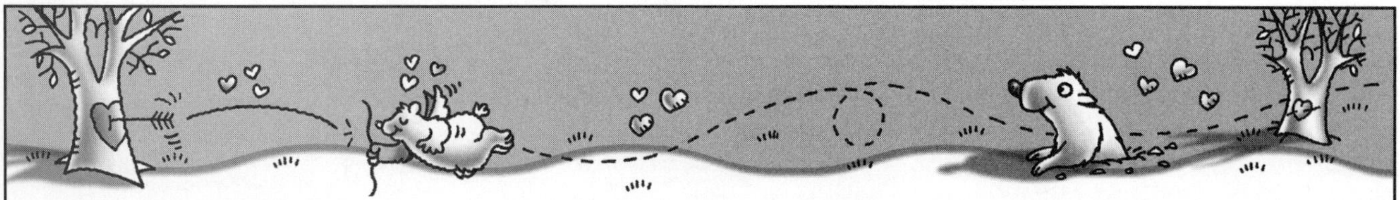

This is something to smile about!

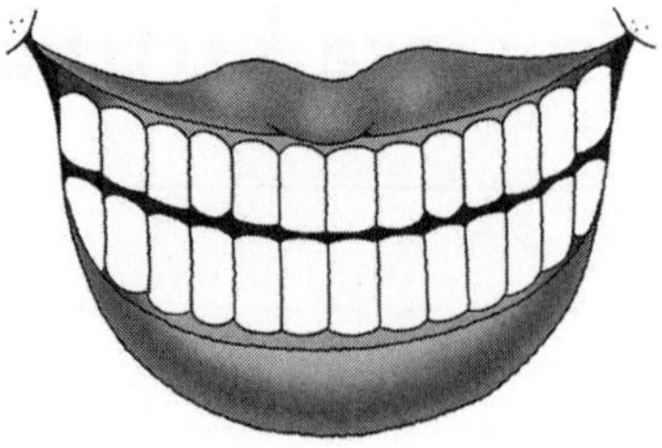

______________________ can ______________________.

Teacher's signature

Date

Calendar Day Pattern

Suggested Uses

- Reproduce one card for each day of the month. Write a numeral on each card and place it on your class calendar. Use cards to mark special days.
- Reproduce to make cards to use in word ladders or word walls.
- Reproduce to make cards and write a letter on each card. Children use the cards to form words.
- Reproduce to make cards to create matching or concentration games for students to use in activity centers. Choose from the following possible matching skills or create your own:
    - uppercase and lowercase letters
    - pictures of objects whose names rhyme, have the same beginning or ending sounds, contain short or long vowels
    - pictures of adult animals and baby animals
    - numerals and pictures of objects
    - number words and numerals
    - colors and shapes
    - high-frequency sight words